Advance Praise for
THE COMMODIFICATION OF AMERICAN EDUCATION:
PERSISTENT THREATS AND PATHS FORWARD

"It's a story that needs telling and this book does that very readably! It's especially useful to those who may disagree with its underlying viewpoint. Especially at this time of peril we need to understand the connections—and misconnections—between schools and democracy!"

–Deborah Meier,
Leader in Holistic Reform in Urban Public Education,
www.deborahmeier.com

"For decades the forces of neoliberalism have sought to make education into a competitive marketplace, turning teaching and learning into a product for profit. *The Commodification of American Education* not only highlights how this has transformed us as people and attacked our very identities, it also shows how we can resist it through tactics of play, unionization, and the reclamation of ourselves as learners. In *The Commodification of American Education*, editors Brewer and Harman have offered a powerful collection to help us all navigate and survive these troubling times."

–Wayne Au, Ph.D., Professor,
University of Washington Bothell
Editor, Rethinking Schools, Teaching for Black Lives,
and author of *A Marxist Education*

"This book not only problematizes the issues across the landscape of education to inform the reader, but it also inspires action. The editors open the discussion by relaying that a resistance movement is challenging the neoliberal paradigm and is opposing the commodification of students and teachers. They urge the reader to bring schools 'under the care of professional teachers rather than leaving it in the hands of people who have never taught students.' Readers will come away with not only with a better understanding of alternatives to neoliberal education reform, but will also glean, in each chapter, more humane ways forward for children, their families, and communities."

–Julian Vasquez Heilig, Ph.D.
Dean and Professor of Educational Policy Studies and Evaluation,
University of Kentucky

THE COMMODIFICATION OF AMERICAN EDUCATION

THE COMMODIFICATION OF AMERICAN EDUCATION

PERSISTENT THREATS AND PATHS FORWARD

EDITED BY
T. JAMESON BREWER
AND
W. GREGORY HARMAN

Myers Education Press
Gorham, Maine

Myers Education Press

Published by Myers Education Press, LLC
P.O. Box 424
Gorham, ME 04038

Myers Education Press is an academic publisher specializing in books, e-books and digital content in the field of education. All of our books are subjected to a rigorous peer review process and produced in compliance with the standards of the Council on Library and Information Resources.

Library of Congress Cataloging-in-Publication Data available from Library of Congress.

13-digit ISBN 978-1-9755-0435-9 (paperback)
13-digit ISBN 978-1-9755-0434-2 (hardcover)
13-digit ISBN 978-1-9755-0436-6 (library networkable e-edition)
13-digit ISBN 978-1-9755-0437-3 (consumer e-edition)

Printed in the United States of America.

All first editions printed on acid-free paper that meets the American National Standards Institute Z39-48 standard.

Cover design by Teresa Lagrange

DEDICATION

TJB: For my first teacher, my father, who taught me that the things in life that matter most are the things that cannot be measured or commodified.

WGH: For all my students whom I know carry forward the most important ideas we shared, none of which were ever on the test.

CONTENTS

Foreword xi
BY NOAH DE LISSOVOY

1. Introduction 1
BY W. GREGORY HARMAN

2. Education and School: How Defining Our Terms Determines Our Approach 13
BY W. GREGORY HARMAN & MATTHEW J. HAYDEN

3. Resisting Neoliberal Reforms in Early Childhood Education: Play Pedagogy as the Antidote to GERM 39
BY DENISHA JONES

4. How Schools Reinforce Socially Constructed Notions of "Smartness" and How We Can Subvert Them Through Trust 63
BY T. JAMESON BREWER & SCOTT T. GRUBBS

5. Creating and Commodifying the Neoliberal Self: A Weberian Analysis of an International Education Course 87
BY ASHLEE B. ANDERSON & ANDREA ARCE-TRIGATTI

6. Combating the Commodification of Knowledge: The Maker Movement 107
BY MICHAEL SCHAD & KURT STEMHAGEN

7. Unionizing Educators in Charter Schools: A Case Study of the Chicago Teacher's Union Organizing Model 125
BY MICHELLE STRATER GUNDERSON

8. What Are "Soft Skills," and Should We Be Teaching Them? 141
by Bailey B. Smolarek

Editor and Contributor Biographies 163

Index 167

FOREWORD

by Noah De Lissovoy

The capitalist market, both as a political and economic space and as an ideological frame, asserts itself as the decisive force shaping contemporary schooling. The fracturing of educational opportunity through funding inequities and as a result of the proliferation of charter schools is celebrated as liberatory and innovative. Meanwhile, as "results"-based accountability seeps deeper and deeper into the educational culture, many schools in the United States give even the youngest children numerical scores on academic and behavioral criteria. Alternative certification programs for teachers, built on threadbare curriculum and racist assumptions about students, are lauded by reformers for challenging the so-called monopoly on teacher preparation held by universities. The ostensibly generous efforts of philanthropists transform schools into laboratories and branding opportunities for big technology. And rigid, behaviorally oriented pedagogies aimed at controlling the bodies of Black and Brown students are praised for fostering responsibility in vulnerable populations that have to learn to make the grade, we are told, in a society that must be ruthless in holding everyone to account.

The turn to the market as the guiding paradigm for education is now decades old. The effort to reframe educational processes and outcomes in terms of bottom lines, value added, and return on investment has been a shared project of elites across the official political spectrum, uniting Democratic and Republican administrations. Furthermore, the punishing regime of high-stakes test-based accountability that has been perhaps the primary expression of the *businessification* of education has survived the concerted opposition of teachers, communities, and scholars, not to mention its own clear failures in raising achievement even according to its own narrow metrics. At present, it is instructive that the Trump administration's putative opposition to the "deep state" and this administration's hard right turn in ideological terms have not shaken the governing neoliberal logic of schooling, even as the administration has simultaneously worked to siphon dollars from the public system to private schools and erode civil rights protections. The commodification of education, it would seem, has moved from being a political goal of insurgent entrepreneurs and policy elites to constituting the very matrix of intelligibility of the meaning of schooling.

What accounts for the durability of this market-based reframing of education? Partly this consistency is the result of education's links to the broader ideological landscape of neoliberalism, with its powerful disqualification of every alternative to market-based orientations to policy. In this context, being rational and *realistic* means acceding to the business model as the foundation for social life (Fisher, 2009). Self-perpetuating neoliberal public–private bureaucracies (in the areas of testing, curriculum design, and teacher preparation) anchor this encompassing common sense for educators and the public alike. We can also point to more explicitly economic forces to the extent that the effort to commodify education is connected to a far-reaching offensive by capital since the 1980s to seize policy initiative and terrain away from working people and social-democratic trends (Harvey, 2005) and to a long-run restoration of the concentration (and rule) of wealth in capitalist societies (Piketty, 2014). In fact, the market-based framing of education opens up crucial opportunities for monetizing governance, teaching, and assessment. In addition, we can understand the commodification of education in the context of a broader shift in the composition of capital itself, which increasingly depends on knowledge and information work across broad sectors of the economy (Hardt & Negri, 2004).

As important as all these explanations are, they also risk losing sight of the specifically *pedagogical* dimension of neoliberalism in education. Education is a crucial site of the market-based reframing of society above all because of the decisive role the classroom plays in organizing selves and relationships. We usually think of this in terms of values and dispositions: teaching sets out hegemonic common senses for students, such as individual responsibility and conflict avoidance (Apple, 2004), as well as inculcating class-based orientations to institutions and authority (Anyon, 1980). Framing learning and achievement in terms of a business model reinforces this process—for instance, as students are taught that they alone are responsible for their success or failure in the free market of education. However, it is important to see that the work that pedagogy does for neoliberalism goes much deeper than privileging certain values or beliefs. Teaching also sets the habits, grammars, and structures of feeling within which subjectivity—our very personhood—is shaped. In this context, the accountability regime is not only an ideological process but also a training of the self. We become *test-takers to the bone*, as it were, as the proliferating official moments of assessment in school spread out to become continuous with forms of audit and surveillance that organize work life, public space, and social relationships of all kinds. In this context, anxiety is not just an occasional internal experience but, rather, an omnipresent and structural feature of contemporary capitalism as well.

The depth of the market paradigm in education, which organizes ways of knowing and being in addition to values and beliefs, means that it can encompass not only authoritarian and back-to-basics modes of teaching but also progressive and "authentic" ones. Indeed, one of the powerful innovations of neoliberalism, as a specific mode of capitalism, is its flexibility: It is expressed in forms of labor and learning built around a certain kind of creativity and collaboration as well as in those defined by routinization and isolation (Boltanski & Chiapello, 2005). Indeed, the case made by neoliberals for charter schools, alternative pathways to teacher certification, and even performance-based rewards and punishments rests on evoking the ideas of autonomy and innovation; the market is supposed to emancipate us from outmoded practices and systems. Of course, freedom and creativity, within the market paradigm, must ultimately prove themselves in the results that they produce and have meaning only in a larger context of competition. The important point is that in the neoliberal era, the logic of the market often envelops even our most "human" and intimate moments, reframing their authenticity as a mode of its own reproduction. This does not mean that constructivist education is not a crucial site of resistance to the stripped-down forms of teaching that market-oriented reformers favor, but it does mean that we have to pay careful attention to the way that the soft skills, teamwork, and "grit" fashionable in schools today are deeply connected to modes of affective and communicative labor required of workers in the contemporary gig economy.

In this regard, the focus in this book on the process of commodification itself in education, not just on dominant values and orientations, is urgent. In the current historical moment, we are living through a process in which more and more of life is being subsumed into the commodity form and the circuits of capital. Emotional labor (in the service industries), "cognitive capital" (in information and technology), and the monetizing of human genetic information (in bioengineering) are some important examples. Marx analyzed the way that the seemingly autonomous form of the commodity as *object* (as in, for instance, a product on the grocery store shelf) conceals the fact that the commodity is produced through a social *relationship* of exploitation (of workers by owners). In the era of service work, this formula is, in a way, inverted so that very often what appears as human and natural *interaction* (e.g., friendly banter with the Starbucks barista) conceals its *objective* status as a commodity (as part of the experience purchased by the customer). This objectification of human relationships and capacities is a key feature of schooling in the neoliberal era, as even nonacademic dimensions of personhood (for both teachers and students) are surveilled and scored—as can be seen, for instance, in the notorious behavioral controls of "no-excuses" charter schools (Darder, 2014).

The chapters in this book urgently illuminate key sites and moments of this process—showing how mind and understanding in school become framed as sets of test scores (or score potentials), how the flat and oppressive science of "reform" violates childhoods, how old essentialisms are reconfigured to construct learning in terms of the production of human capital, and how the system aggressively disciplines teachers as workers, even as administrators seek to present the specialness of the school community as transcending vulgar concerns about pay and labor conditions. This book's intellectual interventions help us to understand—in theoretical terms and in concrete settings of practice—both the ideological mystification that secures the rule of the business model in education and the reorganization of students' very subjectivities produced by the discourses and rituals of neoliberal schooling. This volume also helps us see how the already-distorted rationality of capitalism is stretched even further in the context of contemporary education, as the proliferation of the accountability regime becomes its own justification and as its impoverished bottom-line logic of "performance" and "results" is equated with reason itself.

Do the current shocks to the system created by the COVID-19 pandemic and recent uprisings for racial justice create openings for a kind of education beyond the market-based paradigm that dominates contemporary schooling? In many places, high-stakes standardized tests have been temporarily suspended, previously an almost unthinkable development. Schools have found themselves having to depend on parents to interpret and execute remote learning assignments, and in some cases, parents, with a new sense of agency, have taken the opportunity to create their own learning experiences outside the imaginative boundaries of the mainstream curriculum—although access to the time and technology to take advantage of this opportunity is very inequitably distributed. At the very least, the shift to remote and home-based education has demonstrated that the sites and schedules of learning are not sacred or unchangeable (Love, 2020). In addition, the uprisings in the wake of the murder of George Floyd have inspired many teachers to resist the regimented and Whitestream curriculum enforced by state standards. These uprisings, and the disruptions caused by the pandemic, have created ample opportunity to reflect on the extent to which regular schooling is an assaultive and demoralizing experience for students of color, many of whom are not eager to "get back to normal." Furthermore, all of these events press us to move beyond simple critique and ask, "What other ways of being and understanding, what other forms of imagination and relationship, what other sensibilities and practices might be possible if they weren't foreclosed by neoliberal schooling?"

However, we should not underestimate the power and opportunism of elites and the market-based education to which they are committed. Even the novel kinds of teaching that have emerged in this moment of disruption have been quickly recuperated by state authorities and their curricular frameworks. Likewise, the White supremacy that accompanies and undergirds neoliberalism has shaped schooling continuously from its origins and will withstand any historical accidents (Grande, 2004). As the authors of the chapters in this book show, to move beyond the market as the organizing framework for education, we will need to build an organized movement of resistance within and beyond schools. This movement has to be founded on a solid analysis of the meaning of education in capitalism broadly, and, more specifically, of the flexible logic of neoliberalism, and it has to be clear regarding its targets and purposes. One important danger at this particular juncture: In the context of a growing right-wing "post-truth" and paranoid politics, proponents of market-based accountability and reform may present neoliberal schooling as a bulwark against irrationalism and as a way to shore up the familiar and harmonious policy consensus. We need to reject this argument and the status quo it seeks to uphold, not least because it is the failure of the "free" market to provide security, solidarity, and meaning that is the principal condition that has enabled the rise of authoritarian political formations in the United States and globally.

Only being audacious in imagination and struggle will allow us to push past the limits of a commodified form of education. The red-state rebellions of teachers in recent years, the Movement for Black Lives, and growing anti-capitalist currents can inspire us and point the way forward. These movements refuse the political and cultural consensus of Whiteness and neoliberalism, and they reject the timid civility of liberal social justice gestures. At the same time, these public projects need to be connected to classroom pedagogies that not only critique but also *break with* the rituals of market-based reform. The calls by contributors to this volume for a creative agency for students unrestricted by the stultifying limits of the official standards are urgent in this regard, especially when this agency is supported by the conscious and informed commitment of teachers to challenge norms of school governance, epistemological foreclosures underlying curriculum, and the distorted ethics of relationships in schools—as other chapters in this book describe. *The Commodification of American Education* offers indispensable starting points for what has to be a collective project among educators and community members to remake the meaning, purpose, and organization of teaching and learning. Inspired by these insights and suggestions, the movement against market-based education can perhaps become as exhilarating as it is difficult, and we might find in the experience of struggle itself the sustenance needed to persist in our vision of an (educational) world beyond exploitation and domination.

References

Anyon, J. (1980). Social class and the hidden curriculum of work. *Journal of Education, 162*(1), 67–92.

Apple, M. W. (2004). *Ideology and curriculum* (3rd ed.). RoutledgeFalmer.

Boltanski, L., & Chiapello, E. (2005). *The new spirit of capitalism* (G. Elliott, Trans.). Verso.

Darder, A. (2014, November 30). *Racism and the charter school movement: Unveiling the myths*. Truthout. https://truthout.org/articles/racism-and-the-charter-school-movement-unveiling-the-myths/

Fisher, M. (2009). *Capitalist realism: Is there no alternative?* Zero Books.

Grande, S. (2004). *Red pedagogy: Native American social and political thought*. Rowman & Littlefield.

Hardt, M., & Negri, A. (2004). *Multitude: War and democracy in the age of empire*. Penguin Press.

Harvey, D. (2005). *A brief history of neoliberalism*. Oxford University Press.

Love, B. (2020, April 29). Teachers, we cannot go back to the way things were. *Education Week*. https://www.edweek.org/leadership/opinion-teachers-we-cannot-go-back-to-the-way-things-were/2020/04

Piketty, T. (2014). *Capital in the twenty-first century* (A. Goldhammer, Trans.). Harvard University Press.

Chapter One

INTRODUCTION

by W. Gregory Harman

The authors of this book concur that there is a problem with schooling in the United States. In the chapters, each author reflects on different faces of this same problem, offers explanations, and posits solutions or, at least, paths forward. Each author names the face of the problem they are confronting a bit differently. Jameson Brewer and Scott Grubbs locate credentialism as the engine for a reductionist view of merit, interpreted as smartness (Labaree, 1988, 1997a, 1997b; Maier, 2012). Denisha Jones offers means of recovering from GERM (Global Education Reform Movement) that has invaded early childhood education (Jones, 2017; Wasmuth & Nitecki, 2017). Greg Harman and Matthew Hayden describe neo-essentialism, the schooling ideology that propagates the problem (Imig & Imig, 2006; Kessinger, 2007, 2011). Ashlee Anderson and Andrea Arce-Trigatti point out manifestations of the problem as new managerialism, part of neoliberalism: standards, accountability, and competition. They describe how student teachers, having lived within this paradigm and discourse, tacitly accept it to the extent that other approaches become difficult to practice (Apple, 2005; Spring, 2015, 2017), although they offer some alternatives so we can start. Michael Shad and Kurt Stemhagen, to frame their proposal for improving school with the maker movement, note how standards and accountability have resulted in anti-educational and even dishonest school practices. Michelle Gunderson focuses on teachers' encounters with corporate charter schools and the wider assumption of a business model. Bailey Smolarek, in her exploration of soft skills, illustrates how cultural capital, a concept intended to highlight cultural values, gets reduced to human capital, an approach that renders society only as market and individuals solely as consumer and producer.

Commodification, the theme of this book, is one name for the larger problem with which all the authors are contending. Commodification is the rendering of people or things into items of economic exchange, reducing humans and humanity into objects, and attaching human value to economic metrics.

To see why it is such a problem, we need to take a moment for a primer on subjects and objects. We do not mean the grammatical sense of these terms or the use of subject as belonging to (such as subjects of the United Kingdom). Rather, we mean the place of beings in terms of their meaning and value. In addition to exploring how meaning and value are assigned, it is worth understanding *who* is assigning such value and *why*.

Everything in the universe is a subject unto itself. Ferdinand de Saussure (1916/1998) pointed out that language influences us to forget this. The nouns we use are mere labels that group what are really unique entities. That which we name, put a signifier to, is not the thing itself, the signified. Calling my pet a cat merely associates the unique individual with a nonunique group. Even to tell you that his name is Leonidas, while allegedly pointing at his individuality, is actually another convenient and more specific way to point at him, not a way to encompass his meaning as a unique living being.

This idea about how we must be cautious and consider how words do this to us was not original to de Saussure. The Jewish faith expressed this concept in terms of God thousands of years ago. In their belief, the Word may be the sole means to know God, but there is no word that is the name of God. God is merely a label, a title. The faith is adamant that any word we use for God is a signifier, never the signified. We can see that demanding such a difference for what is sacred is valuable. Mere words cannot capture the sacredness that is in the *living subject*. Every living being is such a subject, and even nonliving entities often are better understood as subjects. This means that they have innate, self-contained meaning and value. They are who or what they are in a complete sense, without reference to others.

An object is anything that we use. To objectify is to render a subject into the value not in and of itself but into value for the use of others. For instance, a tree is a living being, and each one is a unique entity, a subject of its own. When someone looks at it and sees the lumber, they will get from it, the tree has been rendered into an object. Human beings are expert objectifiers. Anything or any person to whom we have access or even mere notice, we can objectify, and we most often do. Sometimes this is not harmful to the subject's unique value, but quite often, it is. A word for objectification at the expense of the person or thing objectified, harmful to its subject nature, is *exploitation*.

A particular form of exploitation is commodification. This means understanding and using a being particularly as an economic object, as an item of exchange to realize profit. To say that the current problem is commodification means that we are in a situation in which every stakeholder, agent, and aspect is framed and treated in terms of a material exchange value rather than in terms of their self-meaning and value as subjects, as ends in themselves.

In schooling, we see this commodifying paradigm everywhere we look. It is there in the most direct and obvious ways, such as corporations seeking to make a profit from children's needs in an entire range of ways, from curriculum materials to tests to vouchers to charter schools (Schneider, 2016). It is also there in less direct contexts, such as the application of all the facets of the business model to schooling and faith in quantitative measurement to capture education. The idea that schooling operates most effectively and efficiently when school is viewed as a paid service offered to parents as consumers is straight from the business model. Many school districts no longer have superintendents but, rather, chief executive officers who are atop the bureaucratic hierarchy and who often use business and economic terms such as *return on investment* when discussing policy. Within this sort of school-as-business, teachers are managed as laborers by applying standards and measurements and held "accountable" to the "outcomes" as determined by high-stakes standardized tests (Hall & Stahl, 2012; Nichols & Berliner, 2007; Ravitch, 2014; Stedman, 2011; Waldow, 2005; Webb et al., 2009). Also, the idea that the credential—a diploma or degree—is the ultimate goal of schooling because of its utility in getting a job stems from that model (Brewer & Potterton, 2020; Labaree, 1988, 1997a, 1997b; Maier, 2012). The assumption that competition is at the center of all human action, as the business world understands it, is presented as commonsensical and beyond question. The commodifying paradigm is necessary for the business model to seem applicable and for the logic to seem obvious. The commodifying paradigm is what makes the current schooling regime possible and to seem desirable.

The problem is not unique to schooling. Rather, it is a manifestation of the materialist cultural trend that launched in the 1980s in the United States and has permeated our society ever since. Most education scholars today identify the beginning of the standards and accountability movement as the publication of *A Nation at Risk* in 1983. This was a report from the U.S. Department of Education that was generated, in part, because President Reagan wished to dissolve the department and eliminate the secretary of education position from the cabinet. The report was dramatic in its language and heightened the drama by extensive misuse of data to paint an artificially dismal picture (Kamentz, 2018). However, it was not the first doomsaying evaluation of American schooling. It is just one of a string of critical reports and evaluations going back as far as the organization of the common schools in the 19th century. Even the recommendations that emerged from it, in and of themselves, were nothing novel. As Mehta (2013) describes, there were at least two other focused, long-term school reform efforts previously that relied upon similar mechanisms. The reason for today's problem is not *A Nation at Risk*, but the singular grip on our schools obtained by one approach following it, a result of a shift in the culture that launched in the 1980s.

The election of Ronald Reagan reflected that the culture was changing, and the leadership of his administration spearheaded the movement. Reagan's aphorism "greed is good" sums up the cultural change most succinctly. The cultural movement tied pre-1960s, dominant-culture values and mores to an ideology of extreme capitalist materialism—as espoused by, among others, Milton Friedman and Ayn Rand. This new conservatism was promoted not merely as an alternative set of ideas to add to the cultural conversation but rather as a *cure* for liberalism, which became shorthand for everything that stemmed from the counterculture of the 1950s and 1960s, both the enlightened elements and the misguided ones (Seib, 2020). Reagan (and, in the United Kingdom, Thatcher) conservatism claimed not to be the same old imperialist capitalism that had triggered the counterculture movements. It would not be the system that abused laborers and used genocide, slavery, racism, and sexism to make a few people vastly wealthy while producing "third-world nations," two World Wars, and the Great Depression. Rather, it was a new form, as advertised by spokesmen such as Friedman, in which classical capitalism, and the elimination of government intervention, would lead to greater prosperity and choice for everyone on Earth. Forty years on, this approach has indeed spurred business to speculative heights that dwarf prior eras, as reflected in the stock and commodity market indices. It can be argued also that it has facilitated the increase in the world economic standard of living overall, although there are counterarguments that the same effect would have occurred without this cult of the market and commodification. It is certain that, rather than generate widespread prosperity, this approach has resulted in the concentration of wealth at levels unimaginable even to the robber barons at the turn of the prior century, as well as to consolidate privilege and maintain systemic oppressions, albeit in subtler forms than their prior incarnations (Pikkety, 2020). However, the story for schools has more to do with what this movement did to change what the culture takes for granted, to believe without question.

Relating this history highlights that the current paradigm of schooling is not inevitable or natural. Paradigm means the assumptions, beliefs, and values by which we interpret and construct. The model that has been in place for schooling, manifested as standards and accountability, corporate charter schools in our urban centers, and so on, comes from a paradigm singularly formed in the crucible of 1980s' conservatism. It is not the way things always have been, nor the way things always have to be. This is important to assert because a frightening facet of the commodifying paradigm is how singular it has become. The language, the assumptions, and the values of that 1980s' conservative movement have become the tacitly accepted norms of our world 40 years later (deMarrais et al., 2019). As they have worked their way past various forms of resistance, they have become not merely an argument for how we should proceed but also a set of assumptions that are unquestionable.

This is not the result of force in the Orwellian *1984* sense. At least it is not yet, although it might go that way. In the year of this writing, the president of the United States converted Homeland Security personnel into extralegal stormtroopers to attack peaceful protestors in Portland, Oregon, and created a commission and funding for an ideologically singular "patriotic" curriculum for the schools (Kanno-Young, 2020; Waxman, 2020). While part of the widespread compliance with commodification certainly has come from increased centralization of schooling policy and funding, up to this point, the new materialism had become a normalized state of affairs without much need for pressure from above.

Rather, it has crept in as the assumed reality, akin to the way society was made compliant in Huxley's *Brave New World*. Much of it comes from the language and behaviors of those who had center stage for schooling matters over this time. While specific elements get described by those people, they have been careful never to label themselves as having a distinct philosophy or being a definite ideological group in their approach to schooling. This is key to having their approach normalized to become "common sense" or "the way things are." They have presented themselves as merely practical and realistic and any alternatives as merely foolish or crazy. They monopolized the discourse without ever pointing it out as one possible discourse, so in accepting it, we lost sight of other possibilities. Foucault (1972) describes this phenomenon as an aspect of discourses: Not only do we frame all experience in terms of the discourse we have, but our imagination can also be locked up by them. In the absence of other discourses to refer to, what is outside our discourse remains outside of our reach, beyond our ability to imagine.

In prior eras, while essentialist views were usually the predominant ones in creating and carrying on schooling, they were part of a healthy back-and-forth with critical and opposing views not only from radical academics but within the policy community and schools themselves as well. There were alternative discourses through which to consider what would be the best schooling and what education really meant. This conversation and competition between approaches came to a standstill as we approached the current century and the federal government's No Child Left Behind revision to the Elementary and Secondary Education Act in 2001. Teacher unions joined into the commodifying paradigm, despite the majority of teachers not really believing in it. School administrators and boards got on the train as well, drawn by what Mehta (2015) calls "the allure of order." Many academics, usually the more quantitatively inclined, clambered on as well, some because it fit their views and others to chase grant money.

This is how we came to where we are, locked in a prison of commodification of students, teachers, concepts, schooling, and education.

There are some opponents of the commodifying paradigm, although their views have been marginalized out of public schooling (for instance, the No Child Left Behind Act specified that only quantitative research could be considered in establishing best practices for teaching—qualitative research was explicitly forbidden from the conversation; see Denzin, Lincoln, and Giardina, 2011). The opponents have any number of labels for the monopolizing paradigm of commodification and its faces. Confusingly, they call it both neoconservative and neoliberal. *Neoconservative* refers to the renewal of a conservative focus on military and economic world domination as a central goal. Meanwhile, the term *neoliberal* does not refer to American liberalism but, rather, stems from the traditional British sense of the term: an ideology of open markets and free trade. To say that something is neoliberal is to identify it as ideologically extreme in its view that free markets are the answer to every question. Thus, it is quite likely for people and positions to be both neoconservative and neoliberal at the same time.

Then, various attributes of the materialist and dominating norms are named as they arise: the business model, which then leads to the new managerialism, which in schools is most fully evidenced by the standards and accountability movement and credentialism, which, when propagated worldwide, is named the GERM (Clarke, 2004; Maier, 2012, Wasmuth & Natecki, 2017). GERM's true believers consolidated the various aspects of the materialist movement into schooling, added it to educational essentialism that pre-dated the movement, and integrated big data. They are called neo-essentialists (Harman, 2019; Imig & Imig, 2006; Kessinger, 2007, 2011). These are the faces of the problem addressed in this book.

Remember that paradigms and their discourses are artifices. They are not natural or inevitable limits but self-imposed ones. We can take on different discourses and the limits shift; what was unimaginable becomes available. This is the case for the authors of this book and many of their colleagues and thousands of other people whom Greg Harman and Matthew Hayden, in their chapter, label the Resistance. The Resistance challenges the materialist paradigm, opposes the commodification of students and teachers, and offers more humane ways forward. They do not pretend that their own ideas are novel or unique inventions. Rather, they offer that our society can actualize the best ideas and practices for facilitating people's education in ways that defy commodification, reject objectification, and value our teachers and our children as subjects. We hope that after you read this book and contemplate further, you will become part of the Resistance if you have not already.

This text has been intentionally curated and written to make the language as accessible as possible. We anticipate that the primary readers of this text will be preservice teacher candidates, and we know that academic texts can be obscure and difficult to navigate. We hope that you find the pages that follow useful for your preparation and continually helpful as you enter the profession of teaching. We welcome and encourage you to get in touch with us with any questions, comments, or desire for further dialogue that you have regarding anything in this book. You can reach Jameson Brewer at tjamesonbrewer@gmail.com and Greg Harman at harmanyed@gmail.com.

References

Apple, M. W. (2005). Education, markets, and an audit culture. *Critical Quarterly, 47*(1–2), 11–29.

Brewer, T. J., & Potterton, A. U. (2020). How market forces and erosion of education as a public good drive equity gaps wider. In M. Soskil (Ed.), *Flip the system us: How teachers can transform education and strengthen American democracy* (pp. 82–96). Routledge.

Clarke, J. (2004). Dissolving the public realm? The logics and limits of neo-liberalism. *Journal of Social Policy, 33*(1), 27–48.

deMarrais, K., Brewer, T.J., Herron, B., & Lewis, J.B. (2019). *Philanthropy, hidden strategy, and collective resistance: A primer for concerned educators*. Gorham, MN: Myers Education Press.

Denzin, N.K., Lincoln, Y.S., & Giardina, M.D. (2011). Disciplining qualitative research. *International Journal of Qualitative Studies in Education, 19*(6), 769–782.

de Saussure, F. (1998). *Course in general linguistics* (C. Bally & A. Sechehaye, Eds.; R. Harris, Trans.). Open Court Books. (Original work published 1916)

Foucault, M. (1972). *The archeology of knowledge: And the discourse on language* (A. M. Sheridan-Smith, Trans.). Pantheon Books.

Hall, R., & Stahl, B. (2012). Against commodification: The university, cognitive capitalism and emergent technologies. *TripleC, 10*(2), 184–202.

Harman, W. G. (2019). Schooling as reform: Consolidation and commodification. *The Sojo Journal, 5*(1), 29–41.

Imig, D., & Imig, S. (2006). The teacher effectiveness movement: How eighty years of essentialist control have shaped the teacher education profession. *Journal of Teacher Education, 57*(2), 167–180.

Jones, D. (2017). When all else fails, we must protect childhood. *Global Education Review, 4*(3), 14–16.

Kamentz, A. (2018). *What 'A Nation at Risk' got wrong, and right, about American schools*. NPREd. https://www.npr.org/sections/ed/2018/04/29/604986823/what-a-nation-at-risk-got-wrong-and-right-about-u-s-schools

Kanno-Young, Z. (2020, August 6). Homeland security chief defends deployments in Portland. *New York Times*. https://www.nytimes.com/2020/08/06/us/politics/homeland-security-portland.html

Kessinger, T. A. (2007). Efforts towards national education reform: An essentialist political agenda. *Mid-Western Educational Researcher, 20*(2), 16–23.

Kessinger, T. A. (2011). Efforts toward educational reform in the United States since 1958: A review of seven major initiatives. *American Educational History Journal, 38*(2), 263–276.

Labaree, D. (1988). *The making of an American high school: The credentials market & the central high school of Philadelphia, 1838–1939*. Yale University Press.

Labaree, D. (1997a). *How to succeed in school without really learning: The credentials race in American education*. Yale University Press.

Labaree, D. (1997b). Public goods, private goods: The American struggle over educational goals. *American Educational Research Journal, 34*(1), 38–81.

Maier, A. (2012). Doing good and doing well: Credentialism and teach for America. *Journal of Teacher Education, 63*(1), 10–22. doi:10.1177/0022487111422071

Mehta, J. (2015). *The allure of order: High hopes, dashed expectations, and the troubling quest to remake American schooling*. Oxford University Press.

Nichols, S., & Berliner, D. (2007). *Collateral damage: How high-stakes testing corrupts America's schools*. Harvard Education Press.

Pikkety, T. (2020). *Capital and ideology*. A. Goldhammer, Trans. Belknap Press.

Ravitch, D. (2014). *Reign of error: The hoax of the privatization movement and the danger to America's public schools*. New York, NY: Vintage Books.

Schneider, M. (2016). *School choice: The end of public education?* Teacher College Press.

Seib, G. F. (2020). *We should have seen it coming: From Reagan to Trump – a front-row seat to a political revolution*. Random House Publishers.

Spring, J. H. (2015). *Globalization of education: An introduction*. Taylor & Francis.

Spring, J. H. (2017). *Political agendas for education: From make America great again to stronger together*. Routledge.

Stedman, L. C. (2011). Why the standards movement failed. An educational and political diagnosis of its failure and the implications for school reform. *Critical Education, 2*(1), 1–21.

Waldow, F. (2015). From Taylor to Tyler in No Child Left Behind: Legitimating educational standards. *Prospects, 45*(1), 49–62.

Wasmuth, H., & Nitecki, E. (2017). Global early childhood policies: The impact of the global education reform movement and possibilities for reconceptualization. *Global Education Review, 4*(2), 1–17.

Waxman, O. B. (2020). Echoing decades of fighting over U.S. history classrooms, President Trump announces a push for 'patriotic education.' *Time*. https://time.com/5889907/trump-patriotic-education/

Webb, P. T., Briscoe, F. M., & Mussman, M. P. (2009). Preparing teachers for the neoliberal panopticon. *Educational Foundations, 23*(3–4), 3–18.

Chapter Two

EDUCATION AND SCHOOL: HOW DEFINING OUR TERMS DETERMINES OUR APPROACH

by W. Gregory Harman & Matthew J. Hayden

This chapter is premised in educational philosophy. This is no reason to run scared! It is true that, as an academic discipline, philosophy can be esoteric and opaque. However, in this chapter, there is no demand that you employ formal rules of logic, read Plato in the original Greek, or understand Wittgenstein's analytical framework. Philosophy, at its center, is what its literal translation means: love, appreciation, and care for true knowledge. True knowledge of things comes from exploring them in a considered, thorough way. It means seeing through surfaces and questioning assumptions to arrive at a truer understanding of them. Becoming a teacher who is an education professional, rather than merely a school technician, means coming to understand the key concepts of your profession deeply. You must move beyond conventional definitions of terms and ideas that are used by laypeople to have a professional level of understanding about your vocation. You must philosophize about education.

At the most basic level, this means defining your terms. In philosophy, an adequate definition is one that is clear, complete, coherent, and compatible with people's experiences of it (Barrow, 2010). We take two terms to explore in this chapter: *education* and *school.* We summarize how they are defined by four separate approaches to schooling. Then, we offer an argument for the definitions from among those that we hope will be persuasive or, at least, give you food for thought in your own contemplation.

All of this connects to commodification because poor definitions of education and school can commodify students, teachers, and the content material. Better ways of defining education and school can defy commodification by envisioning students, teachers, and even content as valuable in and of themselves rather than as objects of exchange value. We will show that schooling determined by neo-essentialist imperatives sees teachers and students as objects of exchange value for something else, which actively discourages genuine education, in which teachers and students are valuable in and of themselves.

Most people most of the time use the terms *education* and *school* interchangeably. Asked to define *school*, we tend to say it is the place where people get education, and asked to define *education*, we tend to say it is what we learn in school. In logic, this is called a *tautology*, which means that it is circular. It never tells us about the terms except in reference to one another, so it leaves us without knowing what either one really means.

Separate assumptions about the meaning of education and school are the source of different views of schooling that are generalized under the labels perennialism, essentialism, educational existentialism, and experientialism/holism. These views of schooling are described in many philosophy of education textbooks. We refer you to any of those texts for a more thorough description than what we offer below (see Knight, 2008; Noddings, 2016; Rocha, 2014). However, the bottom line of their different views, and the central controversies about schooling that they create, is captured by their disparate definitions of education and school.

Perennialism

Perennialists believe that education is an infusion of the human experience to the next generation, particularly via the classics of human cultural activity. Their definition is not merely transmission in the sense of memorization and recall; it demands that students become adept at high-level thinking and abstraction developed by contemplating classics thoroughly. School is the forum in which the next generation is taught to appreciate classics and the first place where they are exposed to them.

There are two central criticisms of the perennial approach. First, it is problematized by determining what counts as classic. The perennialist canon contains mostly White, male, Western contributors, although some advocates of perennialism as "cultural capital" have worked to add other voices. Second, despite the stated openness to adding new classics as they emerge, determining an artifact as genuinely classic is a multigenerational process, so the content of perennial curricula mostly precede the mid-20th century.

Perennialism has been a steadily declining influence on schooling over the past century punctuated both by severe criticism and also occasional rises in interest (i.e., the Paideia movement in the 1980s, headed by Mortimer Adler, or the cultural capital approach spearheaded by E. D. Hirsch). Perennialists were fellow travelers with essentialists in creating the curricula of the common schools, but essentialism grew in a different direction.

Essentialism

An essentialist proceeds from the assumption that education is the information contained in the various academic disciplines. School is the means of transmitting that information from teachers, who know it, to students, who do not (Learned, et al., 1920; Null, 2011). This seems to most of us to be the simplest formulation of the definitions. It fits our commonsense interpretation because most of us are socialized into taking these meanings for granted. As with perennialism, these definitions do not necessarily commodify the stakeholders, although the system that they generated has a tendency to do so.

The essentialists were the inventors of our "one best system" (a phrase coined by David Tyack, 1974, in his history of the school system). This is the system that is still almost universal in American schooling today. It relies on a factory metaphor to organize the relationship among teachers, material, and students (Learned et al., 1920; Imig & Imig, 2006; Mehta, 2013). In this system, teachers become laborers, academic content and students become raw resources, and the product is a citizen-worker with a diploma. The essentialist emphasis is on efficiency and its handmaiden, prioritization. The central work of essentialist curriculum production across the 20th century was determining what to teach and, by extension, what we do not have time to teach. It assumes that the central concern of schooling is the selected "important" subject matter. By extension, it is teacher-centered. However, this still objectifies the teacher. The teacher's value is as a vessel containing the material and a technician who applies methods to instill that material in passively receiving students. If not full commodification, this is objectification of each of the stakeholders and even the content becomes objectified; "learning" becomes a currency that provides access to the next level, not a set of experiences that inform a person's identity, character, or potential.

Essentialism dominated the formation and conduct of schools until the turn of the 21st century. As they went, their prioritization efforts parsed material ever more finely to determine what was important to teach. By the 1980s, the focus had gone from subjects to "competencies," which shifted their view of information in their definition of education away from "knowing that" toward "knowing how." While some traditional essentialists are still out there, the explosion in interest in standards, accountability, and the means of making those the centers of schooling produced neo-essentialism.

Neo-essentialism

Neo-essentialism is an outgrowth from essentialism that has been recognized but is not considered yet in most educational philosophy texts (Harman, 2019; Imig & Imig, 2006; Kessenger, 2007, 2011). It is different enough from essentialism that it warrants consideration as a separate category. Neo-essentialism is a weaponization of essentialism, moving it to an empirical, analytical extreme.

To the neo-essentialist, education has become a label for an outcome: competent performance by students on a series of assessments of skills and recall of data. While essentialists focus on knowledge contextualized within academic disciplines, neo-essentialists demand that each area of knowledge be operationalized. This means it has to be analyzed: parsed into discrete skills and packets of data. The reason for this fundamentalist empiricism is that they believe that we are obligated to use big data in our digital age to keep teachers and schools equally accountable for learning outcomes. Therefore, to the neo-essentialist, nothing taught or learned is guaranteed to be real unless it can be quantified. Lost to the evaluation are the countless interpersonal interactions between students and teachers, the manner, tone, and compassion (or lack thereof) shown students by teachers, and the qualitative appraisals that explain who a student might be and why she might be. All of these could contribute to an education. However, they cannot be measured, so, for neo-essentialists, they do not exist. Conducting studies to determine "research-based best practices" and assessing student outcomes on standardized tests can only be viable by operationalizing and quantifying in this way. The process that they want drives the definition of education as a result, rather than first determining what they think education really means, then creating practices and processes to provide it. Education itself becomes an object to their end of having an accountability process, a process that strips education of its educational qualities (Hayden & Harman, 2020).

For the neo-essentialist, school is society's factory in which teachers use research-based best practices to transmit to students the specified skills and data that turn students into successful producers and consumers in a global economy. In this ideology, all the actors and elements are commodified; they are pieces of a machine. Each element is valuable to the extent that it contributes to the economic product (Waldow, 2015).

The teachers are the laborers who must be managed closely because they are assumed to be doing the work as laborers rather than as professionals. This implies that they do the labor for the wage and will therefore do the least work for most reward. Such an arrangement requires overseers and tight accountability measures, or the laborers will try to get away with working less, and this places teachers in the domain of production surveillance, a key feature of economic production (Hall & Stahl, 2012; Webb et al., 2009). Hall and Stahl (2012) show that assessment tools, ostensibly provided to help teachers help their students, have instead become means of surveillance, little different from using a camera to scrutinize workers on a factory floor. The teachers are commodities in this model, merely labor to produce products (Stedman, 2011). The skills and the students are also commodified. They are materials worked on by the laborers, alloyed to create a product: the 21st-century skilled worker. No single student matters in this model, only aggregations of them as their success or failure on the standardized measures appear in the statistics. Even national accreditation of teacher preparation now relies on demonstrating how the teachers from your program are demonstrating that they provide growth in their students' test scores. Neither student nor content are anything but objects in terms of quantified outcomes. Whether Shakespeare's works have something to say to you is of no concern. Did you score well on the literacy skills assessment? That is all that matters. Content and students disappear in the pool of outcomes assessment. With neo-essentialism, you are a commodity as a teacher and as a student, and anything you know is merely valuable to the extent that it can be part of standardized assessment.

The Resistance: Experientialism, Holism, and Educational Existentialism

The opponents of neo-essentialism are variously experientialists, holists, and educational existentialists. These three groups merge into one in their resistance to the neo-essentialist monopoly on schooling, and they are able to share common arguments against it because they define *school* and *education* in similar ways.

The difference between the neo-essentialist definitions and those of the opposition has arisen because neo-essentialism stems from administration and policy making, while the resistance position has been developed mostly by educators: professors in the social sciences, psychology, and education, as well as K–12 teachers. While there are many clever people who know a lot of things who are neo-essentialists, they are almost never experts in fields that provide deep, thorough explorations of the meaning of either school or education. Sociology and anthropology are best positioned to provide insightful definitions of school. Psychology and philosophy are best positioned to tell us how people learn (and how they do not), what portion of that learning could be counted as education and the meaning of education to a person in a life well lived. Professionals in those fields are rarely neo-essentialists, and most have educational views that are experientialist and holist. The daily experiences of teachers similarly incline them to these views rather than neo-essentialist ones. The next sections present definitions of education and schooling premised on experientialism, holism, and educational existentialism. There are differences between these groups, and someone who is purely any one of these may find fault with the definitions that follow according to their particular approach, but taken generally, I believe they would concur with these as consensus definitions in offering an alternative to the neo-essentialist monopoly on schooling.

A Resistance Definition of Education

Education is the knowledge that each one of us has constructed in our lives that we use across various contexts. It is what we know that we use and thereby enrich and expand. It is not everything we have ever learned, because there is no need for separate terms if learning and education (both as nouns) are exactly the same thing. Also, any of us can recall things we have learned, still remembered in some form, that we rarely or never use so that we have forgotten most of the meaning and use of them. What remains of these things is vague and hollow. These things we indeed learned, but they do not count as part of our education, for we do not still have them in any meaningful sense. This implies that education is also not the things we learned in school, since so many of the things learned there fall into this vague, little-used category or have subsequently been forgotten entirely. For that matter, many things we learned far away from school are things we consider vital in our own educations. They help us in various domains in our lives. We can hardly discount every concept that was not acquired in a classroom. Education also cannot be merely the things we learn that relate to a specific domain, such as within academia, or for our jobs or civic duties because there is no knowledge that remains entirely constrained to one place without seeping over into others. We may learn something for our job, but associated concepts or experiences get recalled and employed in other situations outside of that context. The delineations between subjects and skills that are made by essentialists and neo-essentialists are artifices put in place to attempt to prioritize concepts in curricula. They have nothing to do with the way our minds actually learn concepts (Dehaene, 2020). Therefore, a meaningful, true definition of education is that subset of what we have learned that we find useful and use to shape and live our lives. It is, in a sense, the portion of what we know that composes who we are.

Education can involve various things that are not, in and of themselves, education. The education we get can be comprised of every sort of learning we ever experience: direct, trained, instructed, conversational, and traumatic and even includes socialization and indoctrination. In fact, it is impossible that education could occur without some of these other things, but education is more than what each of those things is by itself. It is in the schema, the combination and connection between things we know, that education is made.

The most up-to-date neuropsychology of learning bears out with some precision what Maria Montessori, John Dewey, Jean Piaget, and Lev Vygotsky proposed about the learning process a century ago (Dehaene, 2020; Dewey, 1921; Montessori, 1995; Piaget, 1970; Vygotsky, 1986). Without reviewing an entire course in educational psychology (which you certainly should take), their essential teaching is this: We learn what matters to us.

Because it matters to us in some way—interest, value, offer of reward or threat, love, and so on—we engage in it. Our awareness is tuned to it so that we attend, receive, and perceive, turning relevant stimuli into concepts.

This has no relation, by the way, to the form of action. A field trip is not necessarily any better than a book. That is not what active learning or experiential learning mean. Teachers make and propagate that mistake all the time, so please don't! What experientialism means is that we find something of value, interest, or importance to the extent that we engage in it and involve ourselves in it. Then how much we do so is what primarily determines how much we learn it. We may be glued to a book so that we have trouble putting it down. We might find a field trip pointless and boring. The reverse could be true as well. It all depends on what we find interesting, valuable, or engaging.

Piaget's version of this proposed the mental mechanism of moving from engagement to knowledge. He proposed that coming to know what we engage in has two forms: agreement with what we already knew (assimilation) or revision of what we already knew (accommodation). In either case, what we know is not like papers or pictures in a drawer somewhere but rather is a living network of connections between concepts, which he called schema (Piaget,

1970). Schema theory was an abstraction when he first proposed it, but neuropsychology today supports that our physiological mechanisms of learning indeed work by active, associative networking, and for that matter, some studies have shown different network activations for assimilative versus accommodative learning (Rubinstein et al., 2020). Piaget's interpretation, while general from a neural perspective, is an accurate one.

Vygotsky's extension of Piaget's developmental and cognition theories was that we need language to create the kinds of extensive, complex schema that human beings make. We need words to configure meaning, to contextualize the new within what we already knew, organized in the schema. Therefore, we need "more experienced others" with whom to communicate in order to learn things. Our knowing always involves a dialogue in which we are a participant with ourselves (with what we already knew), the thing with which we are engaged to know, and other people who have experiences to share language about it (Vygotsky, 1986).

Humanity's experiences with teaching and learning in the absence of careful examination led us to a partial and misapprehended view of how this truth about learning works. Such mistakes are easy to make. For instance, it took a long time for people to realize the Earth went around the sun rather than the other way around. In the case of needing language and more experienced others, it is easy to see how we came to think of learning incorrectly. It seemed as though it was like a hose from the mouth of the teacher to the mind of the student or that the student had an empty bucket and the teacher merely filled the bucket by telling what they know. Lecturing and other forms of telling ensconced in these metaphors have traditionally dominated every part of schooling past elementary education. What Vygotsky's group did was to explore how language connects with learning more precisely, and what they described is not a conduit or a bucket but *construction* by the student with material shared by the teacher. While the teacher is still giving something and the student taking it, the immense difference in the metaphors is the activity in the student's mind that makes concepts out of the dialogue. Lectures and other telling can work very well if the student is interested, engaged, and having internal conversation about the connections between what they hear and what they already know and think about. Education is not obtained from being told but constructed from dialogue within and between people to form the concepts that we value.

Education, the learning that we keep and use across contexts, exists because it is the learning for which we employ this dialogue among the three participants (self, concepts, others) most often or most thoroughly. Networks of neurons grow and interconnect more as experience with a concept increases. When we think we are merely recalling a memory, we actually reconfigure and reconstruct it (Gluk et al., 2019). Our knowing of concepts grows richer with each discussion, each application, and relearning. The expansion of learning occurs from each use. Each time, it encompasses more concepts, and pieces of it can be employed as a metaphor across an ever-greater span of domains and concepts. For instance, a physician not only knows about disease and diagnosis, but she also uses this knowledge as an interpretation of her whole world. She configures social life and politics and personal matters by bringing in medical metaphors and models. A carpenter does this with her craft as well, and a teacher with his. Education is the knowledge we use to live with meaning, the part of what we know that is who we are.

Because this is what education is, it follows that every person *becomes more* as they have more of it. We meet our potentials to the extent that we know more, that our education is fuller. This, not merely economic security, is the reason that education is a human right. Offering more education to one another is an essential, humane value. This is why it is idealized, and providing it more and better all the time is part of the rhetoric of every modern society. This view of education is non-commodifying, even anti-commodifying. Teachers matter in their full selves in dialogue with their students. Students matter in and of themselves since the entire goal is to give them more for their own human, individual potential. Each concept available from material matters in its iteration as a living part of the person who has constructed it.

This makes our profession as educators one of the most profound, even sacred, of pursuits. However, in its current form, school has very little to do with providing it.

A Resistance Definition of School (as it currently exists)

School is an institution designed to socialize the population of a society in the interest of that society. To say it is an institution is central to this definition. In sociology, the meaning of the term *institution* varies slightly depending on the theoretical frame employed. The definition of school offered here uses institution as functionalism does. Functionalism examines how agents of various kinds in a society occupy and create the society in functional terms (Crossman, 2020). However, the exploration of school that follows corresponds with how the other major sociological frames, conflict theory and symbolic interactionism, could determine it, so we can safely proceed with a functional frame for the term *institution*. According to functionalism, an institution (more particularly a formal institution) is a group entity (i.e., company, government agency, charity, school, etc.) that (a) survives and thrives and (b) works to maintain and enhance the existing situation of the society, called the *status quo* (Miller, 2019).

From this point of view, school is not there to educate individuals, because that mission has little bearing either on its own thriving or on consolidating the existing status quo. The status quo is the current state of affairs. The definition of education offered earlier—because it is about building, enhancing, and expanding what is known into something new—directly opposes a focus on maintaining the status quo. In fact, it is likely that more educated people—people who become more than they were as their educations progress—pose more potential to threaten than to preserve the existing arrangements.

To illustrate that school is primarily an institution in the functionalist sense, which means that its mission is not education but its own continuation and consolidation of the existing socioeconomic arrangements, we can examine some of the functions school actually performs as opposed to what it purports to be doing.

School sorts us into our occupations, which involves grading and leveling as we pass through. While it does this, it also creates a forum for socialization and indoctrination through which our compliance with the system is assured. The rhetoric of school tells us that the sorting is done to offer the opportunity of more economic prosperity to more people, associating more school learning with more money. One proof that this is not the truth—that school has little agency in changing opportunity—is the ever-increasing number of people who have seized the opportunity for more schooling has had no impact on the concentration of wealth. According to a report from the 2015 U.S. Census Bureau,

> the percentage of the adult population with a bachelor's degree or higher increased steadily from 1940 to 2015. In 1940, 5 percent of adults held a bachelor's degree or higher. By 2015, this percentage had increased more than five-fold to 33 percent. (Ryan & Bauman, 2016, p. 4)

We have successfully provided more schooling to more people, which implies that we should see widespread upward mobility. This means that the total wealth available in society should be diffusing into more hands. However, the reverse is true: Wealth is more concentrated than ever in our history. In the economy of 2020, one person out of 10,000 of us extracts and keeps \$5 out of every \$100 that exists in the economy. That leaves only about 1 cent for each of the rest of us (Gold, 2017). This is a greater concentration than a decade ago, which was a greater concentration than a decade before that, in a trend that has been continuous since the 1980s.

There are counterarguments that upward mobility is still possible while wealth concentration increases, but they rely on a situation in which a lot of new wealth is constantly being created, which is demonstrably untrue for our economy. Wealth is enough of a closed system that an improvement in people's economic status across their lifetimes and across generations is now the exception rather than the rule. School gets us to tacitly accept a lie about upward mobility in our society. The truth is that fewer people every decade are able to purchase homes, to save money for retirement, or to find jobs for which they have gotten their extensive schooling (Kochhar, 2018).

The school system is not merely neutral in limiting upward mobility but is one of the culprits. Research by Garcia and Weiss (2017) has shown that "children's social class is one of the most significant predictors—if not the single most significant predictor—of their educational [in our terms, schooling] success" (p. 1). The gaps determined by social class take root in the earliest years and do not close. As Garcia and Weiss put it, "children who start behind stay behind—they are rarely able to make up the lost ground" (2017, p. 1). The lack of primary schooling success leads to a lack of secondary schooling success, which leads to a third level of schooling inequality: Those wealthier students are more likely to gain admission to colleges and universities, further compounding the economic inequalities created and maintained by the schooling system. Our own march through school as children, the rhetoric of opportunity, and reform allegedly aimed to provide equal schooling all indoctrinate us to take for granted a lie about upward mobility. There are other such lies designed to protect school itself and the societal status quo that we accept simply because school tells them to us.

For instance, the constant call for more "STEM (science, technology, engineering, mathematics) education," which translates to a demand for more resources for ever-increasing science and math curricula, allegedly comes from a shortage of STEM professionals that the society needs. This is a myth (Anft, 2013). Although debunked by several studies as far as a decade back, the myth continues to be propagated. The primary source of the calls for STEM graduates are STEM employers who want to maintain a buyer's market, which keeps the compensation lower for their workers and leaves a lot of qualified workers worldwide without jobs in their fields. The myth continues to succeed because it fits and reinforces the cheerful narratives we have about our economy and society. This, added to its appeal as job insurance for STEM instructors, makes it practically impossible to dislodge. Note how this situation fits with the neo-essentialists' commodified view of education: It is employers who are propagating this myth about schooling products (people as workers) to gain financial advantage. The myth of the STEM worker shortage is a manipulation of supply and demand to reduce the cost of labor as trained in the schooling system. This is a direct commodification of schooling purposes and products.

The disjunctions among the rhetoric, policy, and reality of schooling happens because school is meeting its institutional mandate to survive and thrive itself and to serve the status quo. It survives and thrives inasmuch as we believe we need school to guarantee the upward mobility that we falsely believe it produces. It reinforces the status quo by feeding our societal narrative of upward mobility and endless personal possibilities for each individual, an essential filter for our sense of appropriateness and justice.

Connected to this, the common grading and promotion approaches of school keep us from complaining about economic injustice. Grades and level promotions sort success from failure in a way that is clearly not designed as a tool for the teacher to help struggling students. Rather, they create a hierarchy of performance that socializes us to believe that the place we end up is the place we deserve. If you get failing grades in school and stay in basic level courses, then being an hourly paid worker is all that you are to expect. If you get all As in all honors and Advanced Placement courses, then, of course, you are encouraged to get higher degrees, which supposedly will result in a high-paying, salaried career. People between those extremes can expect their socioeconomic life to reflect that in-between status as well. Exceptions to these outcomes, such as the occasional person who becomes a billionaire after dropping out of college, simply highlight the view that success is all about individual qualities rather than opportunity that the system has provided or denied.

Looked at in one way, school is an appropriately meritocratic sorting mechanism. We tend to look at it this way and are reinforced in doing so. However, the inequities in what is provided between different schools and school systems stemming from the preexisting economic, racial, and cultural status of their students provide evidence that it is not really a meritocracy but a means of keeping as many people as possible in the socioeconomic status that their parents already occupy, carrying out the roles that their "sort of people" have traditionally carried out. It also helps to remember that Michael Young, who coined the term "meritocracy," did so to expose the myth of the idea that those who achieve wealth or poverty deserve what they get through their own choices and actions. In his book *The Rise of the Meritocracy*, Young (1958/1994) showed that even if a society was able to achieve a system whereby the smartest and hardest working people ended up on top (IQ + effort = merit) and those who were either stupid or lazy landed at the bottom, the system forces people to internalize their own sense of deserving: If you succeeded or failed, it was because of you. The trap of such a system, as Young saw it, is that subsequent generations of the successful and wealthy have internalized the sense of their deserving and believe it is heritable. They then use their power and influence to gain unfair advantages for their children, thus enshrining the progeny in the upper classes whether they deserved it or not. This also keeps the potentially deserving children of the poor mired in poverty. The meritocracy undermines itself because of the sense of deserving what we get. We see this precise effect in our society through the sorting that we do between school districts and within schools that reinforce the advantages of the wealthier families and the disadvantages of the poorer families, consigning them to a socioeconomic track with little attempt to help their children cultivate their merits. The result is that so-called meritocratic institutions like schools serve to promote the status quo by dissolving merit in a solution that provides an appearance of legitimate and fair processes open to all.

The rhetoric and universal presence of school are there to keep us believing that there are wonderful possibilities in store for us as long as we succeed in what school asks. The corollary to this is that, when we do not succeed in school, our tendency is to blame ourselves, which is exactly what the system (and meritocratic thinking) requires for compliance and thus continuity. It is a combination of sorting, socialization, and indoctrination that school continues to serve brilliantly. Schools continue and the status quo is maintained, and those two things are what school is really for.

There are other elements of school functioning as an agency to propagate itself and maintain the status quo that have been thoroughly described over the past 50 years, including the idea of the hidden curriculum (a term coined by Philip Jackson, 1968/1990, in his classic *Life in Classrooms*, which we recommend. Other writers who have explored the hidden curriculum include Freire, 1970/2000; Postman & Weingartner, 1969; and Spring, 2017). The essence of this concept is that the academic material of school is not where the real lessons are learned, nor is it the true expectation of schooling that they are. The true intention is that we are all trained into the routines of living in a mass society: coming and going in orderly ways according to someone else's instructions, complying with authority in its often ridiculous as well as its legitimate demands, and so on. We all live through school and learn the games of getting through it successfully. While we often believe that we are managing or even fooling the system, the outcome is that it trains us to be and do what society wants us to be and do. Even the self-identified rebels among us have created that identity in opposition to what we learned in school and are thus just as much a product of it as anyone else. And most rebels in our society resist the status quo on the margins, rarely in a substantial way. We are what we have become through schooling. As with work lives, even our habits and means of getting through become differentiated based on our sex, our color, and our culture in the compliance factory of schooling. All of it assures the continuance of school and reassures that our socioeconomic arrangements will not be challenged by demands for greater social justice.

It is important to note that these are features of the functional movement of the whole society. None of these elements are formulated by some cabal of conspirators to result in the indoctrinating and socializing functions they perform. Our media today often leads us to view issues in terms of good guys and bad guys, in which the success of the bad guys is explained by nefarious conspiracies. Yet none of this requires conspiracy. Society constructs institutions to meet its needs tacitly and with the best of intentions, not as a matter of purposeful oppression. Certainly, people's own perceived interests guide their values and their goals. This means that there are *some* people who knowingly work for ends that are not in society's best interest. However, it is far more common that the agents of negative outcomes are working hard for what they believe is best. This is the situation for most teachers and other education professionals. By working within schools, with the priorities that schools have, the structure they assume, and relying on things like "research-based best practices," teachers carry out the work of school as a functional institution: sorting, socializing, and indoctrinating students. Our care and intentions notwithstanding, we become agents of the institution serving the status quo.

How School Is Anti-Educational

Using these definitions, it becomes clear that education neither depends on school, nor is it mutually exclusive from school. It is what we are told school is there to provide, and although it is not what school is really designed to produce, we can certainly obtain some education there. Some people are offered more that is valuable for their own education than others in school. However, there is a way in which the process of school becomes anti-educational as experienced by most students.

The structure of schooling is a deterrent to the kind of genuine, interested engagement with ideas that comprises education. Most of us, presented with the mandates of school, learn how to manage what it expects so as to get through as we are required to. We learn school as a game. Game theorists tell us that, in being the competitive and cooperative social beings that we are, we interpret every social situation as a game with rules and that we figure out how to negotiate the game in the most efficient way for our own ends (Case, 2008).

In the school game, most of us figure out quickly that our interest and engagement are not the most efficient way to get through. The game is about getting along and passing assessments. We learn all the ways to pass various forms of evaluation with the minimum expenditure of effort or involvement. In the psychology of problem-solving, this is called distance-reduction, and it is a powerful tendency in most creatures. This makes sense, because in survival situations, seeking out minimum effort for maximum results is vital. However, for education, it is toxic. The easiest way to get through school is precisely to avoid interest, engagement, or involvement, and yet these are precisely the elements required for education to occur. The game of school is the game of promotion to the next level, to obtain the qualification. School is pursued for its utility in giving us what we're really after at the end of it, not for what we are given to know *within* it. School becomes only incidentally connected to what we learn such that we remember it and use it across contexts in our lives. The school game is not mutually exclusive from education, but when we see school as a game of succeeding qualifications, it works against finding education there.

For instance, consider the course for which you are reading this. If you are like most teacher candidates, you are striving for a B– or better to make it through the program to get a degree and license to teach so you can get a teaching job. If you desire high marks and/or are conscientious as a student generally, you will read with some attention and perhaps take some notes. However, because your motivation was utility-based rather than intrinsic, no matter what these pages contain, you likely will not remember it. Then, in surveys, principals will say that the teachers come to them without knowing various things, which seems to confuse the professors who design and run the preparation programs because they know that they *taught* all those things at least twice. Of course, the professors should not be confused because we are supposed to know both how schooling is conducted and how learning happens and should all be aware by now that the former practically ensures that the latter will not occur.

Since you were in first grade, you were in a system that valued promotion to the next level based on the evaluation of discrete skills. What you cared to learn was a marginal component that some teachers may have paid a bit of attention to. Their central goal was to be able to promote you to the next grade in good conscience. The main question for both the teacher and for you was whether you performed adequately on literacy and numeracy skills assessments. Your job, in short, has been to pass assessments. By the time you have entered your teacher education program, your entire schema for how it is all configured practically guarantee that you will take every path of least resistance to your degree and license, which pretty much assures that you will not know much that was taught within your courses (are you still reading?).

You may take for granted that your success at the school game is a fine thing, but as teachers, we all get punished and not just because we start teaching without knowing all we might. More important, each of our students experiences school the same way we did, so our honest attempts to get them to know things that we want them to know will be just as frustrated as our own teachers' and professors' attempts with us. No matter what reform we implement, most students resist taking much from the curriculum. In a century and a half of mass schooling that has purported to educate people, it has never done so for most students. We continue to spend billions of dollars on our K–12 and undergraduate educational efforts in the society, when we know with some certainty that people are not actually learning the bulk of what was taught (Stedman, 2011).

This illustrates that school as an institution does not have education as its primary function. Rather, it exists to sort, socialize, and indoctrinate, and any education obtained is, at best, an unintended consequence. In the matters for which it is really designed, it is highly successful, so it persists. The school game benefits the status quo to the extent that most of us apply it to the rest of our lives. School is outstanding at teaching us to figure out how to get through hurdles with minimal engagement. We learn quite well how to be patient enough to tolerate all sorts of ridiculousness in our work and civic lives to get through. We learn to manage our relationships with what is demanded of us and what authority tells us to do.

The people who do not learn this game and how to apply it elsewhere are considered the outstanding failures of the school system. They are usually labeled with disorders, and they may, in fact, have challenges, but their honest responses when most of us are proceeding with our eyes averted and heads down should perhaps alert us not to their deficiencies but to our own.

By creating winners and losers in a rigged game of acquisition of socioeconomic currency instead of education, schools commodify education. They transform it into indoctrination, marginalizing and discouraging its educational components.

Society needs cooperation from its people, and a mass, complex society with modern economies creates extensive demands for compliance, so there are positive arguments to be made for the socializing and indoctrinating functions of school. However, these have little to do with education, and as teachers, we must be aware that education is a separate matter.

What Is To Be Done?

If you (1) find that these arguments have been compelling, (2) value education as defined in this chapter, (3) believe that your profession as a teacher should be about facilitating peoples' education, and (4) will be trying to do so in a school, you now have a dilemma: How can you educate students when school is organized to discourage it in so many ways? It is simple and is true for everyone in every situation where there is a potential for greater justice: Each of us must do the best we can to make it better.

In the case of a teacher in a school, this means that you will first learn everything that your program has to offer, even methods and approaches that serve the neo-essentialist agenda. You will learn what is being demanded with a critical sensibility of how you will apply it (or not) once you are the professional carrying out the practice. You will know how to use all the tools, including ones oriented toward management rather than community that tend to reinforce the problems, but you will see them as selectively and carefully used tools, not as your purpose.

Then, you will oppose neo-essentialism with its commodification, its standardization, and its shallow accountability. You will resist having your job configured in terms of skills, discrete assessments, and leveled promotion of your students. You will create classroom environments that invite interest and curiosity and that are centered on peace, welcoming, sharing, and kindness. You will use that environment as a forum for rich discussion. You will hear as much from the students as you tell them. You will understand your work as facilitating their understanding, helping to fulfill their search for meaning. You will use subject matter and skills as means to this end rather than as ends in themselves. You will never rely on canned curricula. You will undermine the school game so that they learn not to play it in your class but to pursue their education instead.

You will always be finding out more about the matters you teach them and about matters in your profession. You will be an activist for changing policy so that schools will change, not through some specific reform program but in the interest of student–teacher relationships, dialogue, and invitational approaches. You will be professionally responsible in trying to bring schools under the care of professional teachers rather than leaving it in the hands of people who have never taught students.

If you think about it, the teachers who really did inspire you, whom you remember most fondly, were doing at least some of these things. The teachers you either do not remember or remember with distaste were not. Be the teacher you would love the most, and that will change the meaning of school for your students.

References

Anft, M. (2013). The STEM crisis: Reality or myth? *The Chronicle of Higher Education.* https://www.chronicle.com/article/the-stem-crisis-reality-or-myth/

Barrow, R. (2010). Was Peters nearly right about education? *Journal of Philosophy of Education, 43*(1), pp. 9–25.

Case, J. H. (2008). *Competition: The birth of a new science.* Hill & Wang.

Crossman, A. (2020). *Understanding functionalist theory, one of the major theoretical perspectives in sociology.* Thought Co.

Dehaene, S. (2020) *How we learn: Why brains learn better than any machine . . . for now.* Viking Press.

Dewey, J. (1921). *Democracy & education: An introduction to the philosophy of education.* The Macmillan Co. (Original work published 1916) https://archive.org/stream/democracyeducatioodeweuoft?ref=ol#page/n7/mode/2up/search/reconstruction

Freire, P. (2000) *Pedagogy of the oppressed* (30th anniversary ed.; M. B. Ramos, Trans.). New York, NY: Continuum Publishers. (Original work published 1970).

Garcia, E., & Weiss, E. (2017). *Educational inequalities at the school starting gate: Gaps, trends, and strategies to address them.* Economic Policy Institute.

Gold, H. R. (2017). Never mind the one percent, let's talk about the .01 percent. *Chicago Booth Review.* https://review.chicagobooth.edu/economics/2017/article/never-mind-1-percent-lets-talk-about-001-percent

Gluck, M. A., Mercado, E., & Myers, C. E. (2019). *Learning and memory: From brain to behavior* (4th ed.). Worth Publishers.

Hall, R., & Stahl, B. (2012). Against commodification: The university, cognitive capitalism and emergent technologies. *TripleC, 10*(2), 184–202.

Harman, W. G. (2019). Schooling as reform: Consolidation and commodification. *The Sojo Journal, 5*(1), 29–41.

Hayden, M., & Harman, W. J. (2020). Schoolings relative non-autonomy: Technocratically subordinated schooling and de-sublimated education. *Educational Theory, 71*(1), XX.

Imig, D., & Imig, S. (2006). The teacher effectiveness movement: How eighty years of essentialist control have shaped the teacher education profession. *Journal of Teacher Education, 57*(2), 167–180.

Jackson, P. W. (1968/1990). *Life in classrooms*. Teacher's College Press.

Kessinger, T. A. (2007). Efforts towards national education reform: An essentialist political agenda. *Mid-Western Educational Researcher, 20*(2), 16–23.

Kessinger, T. A. (2011). Efforts toward educational reform in the United States since 1958: A review of seven major initiatives. *American Educational History Journal, 38*(2), 263–276.

Kochhar, R. (2018). *The American middle class is stable in size, but losing ground financially to upper-income families*. Pew Research Center. https://www.pewresearch.org/fact-tank/2018/09/06/the-american-middle-class-is-stable-in-size-but-losing-ground-financially-to-upper-income-families/

Knight, G. R. (2008). *Issues & alternatives in educational philosophy* (4th ed.). Andrews University Press.

Learned, W. S., Bagley, W. C., McMurry, C. A., Strayer, G. D., Dearborn, W. F., Kandel, I. L., & Homer, W. J. (1920). *The preparation of teachers for America's public schools: A study based upon an examination of tax-supported normal schools in the state of Missouri*. New York, NY: The Carnegie Foundation.

Mehta, J. (2015). *The allure of order: High hopes, dashed expectations, and the troubling quest to remake American schooling*. Oxford University Press.

Miller, S. (2019, Summer). Social institutions. In E. N. Zalta (Ed.), *The Stanford encyclopedia of philosophy*. https://plato.stanford.edu/entries/social-institutions/

Montessori, M. (1995). *The absorbent mind: A classic in education and child development for educators and parents* (J. Chattin-McNichols, Ed. & Trans.). Holt Publishers.

Noddings, N (2016). *Philosophy of education*. Abingdon, UK: Routledge.

Null, W. (2011). *Curriculum: From theory to practice*. Summit, PA: Rowman & Littlefield Publishers, Inc.

Piaget, J. (1970). *The science of education and the psychology of the child* (D. Coltman, Trans.). Orion Press.

Postman, N., & Weingartner, C. (1969). *Teaching as a subversive activity*. Dell Publishing.

Rocha, S. D. (2014). *A primer for philosophy & education*. Cascade Books.

Rubinstein, J., Racik, P., Chen, B., & Kwan, K. Y. (2020). *Neural circuit and cognitive development: Comprehensive developmental neuroscience*. Academic Press.

Ryan, C. L., & Bauman, K. (2016). *Educational attainment in the United States: Population characteristics* (Current Population Reports). U.S. Census Bureau.

Spring, J. (2017). *Political agendas for education: From make America great again to stronger together*. Routledge.

Stedman, L. C. (2011). Why the standards movement failed. An educational and political diagnosis of its failure and the implications for school reform. *Critical Education, 2*(1), 1–21.

Tyack, D. (1974). *The one best system: A history of American urban education*. Harvard University Press.

Vygotsky, L. (1986). *Thought & language* (A. Kozulin, Trans.). MIT Press.

Waldow, F. (2015). From Taylor to Tyler in No Child Left Behind: Legitimating educational standards. *Prospects, 45*(1), 49–62.

Webb, P. T., Briscoe, F. M., & Mussman, M. P. (2009). Preparing teachers for the neoliberal panopticon. *Educational Foundations, 23*(3–4), 3–18.

Young, M. (1994). *The rise of the meritocracy*. Transaction Publishers. (Original work published 1958)

Chapter Three

RESISTING NEOLIBERAL REFORMS IN EARLY CHILDHOOD EDUCATION:

PLAY PEDAGOGY AS THE ANTIDOTE TO GERM

by Denisha Jones

In play a child is always above his average age, above his daily behaviour; in play it is as though he were a head taller than himself.

—Vygotsky (1967/2016, p. 18)

Furthermore, why not call play the work of teachers as well? If, as Lev Vygotsky, the Russian psychologist, informs us, children rise above their average behavior in play, let us pursue the ways in which their teachers might follow them up the ladder, starting at the first rung, which, as every child knows is fantasy play.

—Vivian Paley, *A Child's Work: The Importance of Fantasy Play*

There are credible oppositions to the hegemony of neoliberalism. What if "the play movement" looked to these oppositions, to social movements inspired by Black Lives Matter, #MeToo, RedForEd, and all of their diverse and similarly-spirited advocates and agents who live with and around us? What if we seek the appropriation of time,

> space and resources towards childhood in ways that work toward destruction, liberation, and insurgency?
>
> —Ben Dalby, *What Is Playwork Under Neoliberalism?*

The commodification of education often begins in early childhood education through policies often labeled "best practices" or "evidence-based." Taken for granted that these approaches will help all children achieve academically, the commodification of childhood is accepted as natural and normal. If the goal of American education is to produce the highest scores on standardized exams, then it seems natural that we should ensure young children are up to this task. Although No Child Left Behind (NCLB) mandated yearly testing to begin in third grade, many school administrators recognized they could have an edge in the competition for top scores if they begin preparing children in first grade. Thus, kindergarten became the new first grade, where ample time for child-centered play with blocks and art is replaced with literacy and math learning centers and more teacher-directed instruction (Bassok et al., 2016; Miller & Almon, 2009).

The commodification of childhood is an outcome of how the Global Education Reform Movement (GERM) operates in early childhood education. One-size-fits-all standards, high-stakes standardized assessments that begin in kindergarten, and the pushdown of academics in the early years are a few examples of how GERM impacts the early years. However, the language used to push these reforms, sanitizes the discourse, and muddies the reality. Words such as *college and career ready, high quality*, and *developmentally appropriate practices* convey outcomes and experiences we should want for all children. But they fail to reveal that the means used to pursue these ends turn childhood into an object and early learning into a commodity.

To protect childhood, we must resist GERM and all its manifestations in early childhood education. However, resistance is not enough. We must put forth a vision of what it means to protect childhood in our everyday work with children and their families. We must change the narrative on what defines "high quality" and "developmentally appropriate practices" in early childhood education. We must alter our expectations of early childhood teachers from transmitters of knowledge to guardians of childhood. We must redefine what it means to return to the basics from a narrow focus on particular academic skills to a commitment to play, freedom, and liberation.

In this chapter, I theorize how we protect childhood and reclaim our pedagogy as early childhood educators. First, I briefly examine how GERM has caused a global crisis in early childhood education, which has led to an erosion of childhood. Next, I return to the basics of child development and learning: play. I argue that play can inoculate early childhood education from the GERM infestation, focusing on the global true play movement. Finally, I discuss what it means to enact a play pedagogy as a tool for protecting childhood.

GERM And The Global Crisis In Early Childhood Education

At the First Annual True Play Conference held in Anji, China, in 2019, Ms. Cheng Xueqin, director of the Anji Childhood Education Research Center and founder of the Anji Play approach, began her presentation by identifying the five components of a global crisis in early childhood education (Jones, 2019b). As I listened to her presentation, I recognized how each component connected to a feature of GERM (Wasmuth & Nitecki, 2017) (see Table 3.1). Although countries implement reforms in context-specific environments, the underlying push for commodification and standardization are evident throughout the various approaches.

In the United States, the passage of No Child Left Behind (NCLB) by the federal government in 2001 ushered in numerous education reforms with the impetus of standardizing teaching and learning. As a result, kindergarten transformed from a place for child-centered play, hands-on exploration, and development of social skills to the new first grade, where we expect children to learn through a prescriptive teacher-directed curriculum linked to revised state standards (Miller & Almon, 2009; Repko-Erwin, 2017). An increase in standardization leads to a decrease in children's access to deep learning through play. In their report titled *Crisis in Kindergarten*, Miller and Almon (2009) argue that the increase in standards and unrealistic expectations combined with the decrease in play contributes to a rise in reports of severe challenging behaviors. They recommend that those who seek to protect childhood "restore child-initiated play and experiential learning with the active support of teachers to their rightful place at the heart of kindergarten education" (Miller & Almon, 2009, p. 13).

Table 3.1. Features of GERM and Components of the Global Crisis in ECE.

FEATURES OF GERM	COMPONENTS OF THE GLOBAL CRISIS IN ECE
Standardization	The right of children to authentic experiences of deep learning is not part of the design or priorities of current systems.
Focus on core subjects	Current approaches based on outdated view of learning and focus on increasing irrelevant skills
Using prescribed curricula to teach for predetermined outcomes	Lack of access for the most marginalized communities
Insisting on increased control over teachers	Early educators treated as unskilled and unempowered
Test-based accountability	Institutions, organizations, and experts have created and benefit from systems that will not change from within regardless of how they redefine skill sets.

Note: A similar table can be found in my blog *How a True Play Revolution Can Protect Childhood* (Jones, 2019b).

Standardization and test-based accountability result in a narrowing of the curriculum through a focus on literacy and math. Repko-Erwin (2017) notes that NCLB led to a further narrowing of the kindergarten literacy curriculum through a hyper-focus on decoding skills. Not only are subjects like science, social studies, art, and music removed or drastically reduced in early childhood classrooms, but the approach to teaching core subjects is also reduced to isolated skills devoid of a meaningful context, which can be especially harmful to diverse learners (Repko-Erwin, 2017, p. 69). The prescribed curriculum that flows from efforts to standardize teaching and learning is often the only option for marginalized families. Parents with social and economic capital can provide their children with an engaging, child-centered curriculum, often priced out of reach of low-income and poor families.

The mandated use of prescribed curriculum combined with an increase in standardized assessments led to a deprofessionalization of early childhood teachers. Child-centered progressive education prepared early childhood teachers to observe children closely to make curriculum decisions based on the child's interest and development. As teachers are forced into meeting predetermined learning outcomes based on universal standards, their autonomy based on professional experience is replaced by the assumptions of technicians and policy makers who often lack training in child development. Hatch (2002) found an example of deprofessionalization with early childhood teachers in the United States and Australia when their use of observation to influence curriculum decreased and shifted to an increase in monitoring student progress. A scripted curriculum strips teachers of their ability to make decisions in the classroom, thereby tightening control over their actions and constraining their sense of empowerment.

Despite all the concerns with high-stakes standardized tests, they continue to serve a gatekeeper function maintaining public education as a system of winners and losers. Touted as necessary for holding teachers accountable, measuring the school's progress, and closing the "achievement gap,"[1] high stakes standardized testing proliferated with the implementation of NCLB (Nichols & Berliner, 2007; Ravitch, 2013). Nichols and Berliner (2007) note that standardized tests have been around for centuries as have criticisms of their use as high stakes measures. Yet, they persist despite the dire warnings that their use is "paving the way for an educational crisis that threatens to leave our *nation* behind" (2007, p. 7, emphasis in the original).

Standardized assessments become high stakes when they are used to make high-stakes decisions about students and teachers. States that require high school students to pass a standardized test to receive a diploma make standardized testing high stakes. The increasing practice of tying teacher evaluation to standardized test scores reinforces the high-stakes nature of testing throughout K–12 schooling. Although the number of states mandating high school exit exams decreased for the class of 2020 from 27 to 11, the impact of this requirement is still a concern for many students whose entire K–12 careers rest on their ability to pass one test (FairTest, 2019). We must remember that the use of high-stakes standardized tests creates a system of winners and losers, and it is the winners who tend to maintain their faith in standardized teaching, learning, and assessments as best for all children. As long as there are a group of people purported to benefit from high-stakes exams, the system can continue operating as though it serves everyone's best interest when, in reality, its benefits extend only to those who excel at them—plus the test companies and corporations that profit from them. Time and money are expanded to help all children pass tests instead of rethinking whether these assessments are the cause of problems in education and people's lived experience.

The Erosion of Childhood

We conceptualize childhood as a specific period, from birth to puberty or even adolescence, distinct from adulthood. Moreover, childhood is that particular time where young children develop the knowledge and skills needed to become functioning members of society. Changes in society, from hunter-gatherer to agricultural to industrial to globalization, have profound impacts on the role of childhood and the rights and responsibilities of children (Stearns, 2015). Children, and their time to grow, shifted from an emphasis on working to support the family to the need for education to prepare children for the workforce. Stearns (2015) contends that this shift in the conception of childhood also shifted the primary responsibility of childhood from contributing to the family to developing the individual. Through compulsory schooling, society took on more responsibility from the family. Today, the role of school and education has been broadly construed by some to mean preparing children to be college and career ready. However, others argue that education is the institution through which we must prepare youth to create a better and more just world. Despite these two diverse aims, childhood is greatly impacted by the institution of schooling through explicit and implicit means.

Various standards measure childhood by examining factors related to child well-being. These vary from country to country though sometimes they overlap. In her editorial for a special issue on Nordic ideals and educational practices, Wagner (2008) identifies seven central tenants of *the good childhood*, a widely embraced ideal firmly entrenched in policy and practice in Nordic countries (Sweden, Denmark, Finland, Iceland, and Norway). The Berry Street Childhood Institute in Australia identified three broad outcomes and 13 indicators of development across multiple areas that contribute to a good childhood (Berry Street, 2017). The Children's Defense Fund (2020) issues a *State of America's Children* report every few years that analyzes how children are faring based on 11 areas. See Table 3.2 for a comparison of the measures described earlier.

When we focus on the United States, the data reveals a disappointing portrait of childhood. The *State of America's Children 2020* (Children's Defense Fund, 2020) provided these shameful findings:

- Nearly 1 in 6 children—more than 11.9 million—were poor in 2018. Nearly 73 percent of poor children were children of color.
- Income growth for the wealthiest few has far outpaced growth for everyone else. Since 1980, incomes for the top 1 percent of earners have grown by 226 percent compared with only 47 percent for the middle 60 percent of earners.
- Nearly 6 million children live in low-income families that spend more than half their income on rent and get no rental assistance from the government. Only 1 in 4 eligible households receive federal housing aid.
- More than 1 in 6 children—12.5 million—lived in food-insecure households in 2017. The percent of Black and Hispanic households with food-insecure children was nearly two times that of White households. (p. 7)

Table 3.2. Comparison of Measures of Child Well Being in Nordic countries, Australia, and the U.S.

Nordic Countries Good Childhood	• naturalness of childhood • equality and egalitarianism • democracy defined as *lived* daily experience for children • freedom, conceptualized as autonomy to play and to develop one's own self • emancipation, or liberation from over-supervision and over-control by adults • warm and cooperative social relationships with adults and peers • solidarity with Nordicness, or connecting with Nordic heritage…(Wagner, 2008, p. 265)
Berry Street Childhood Institute, Australia	Thrive • Domain: Safety and Security • Domain: Healthy Development • Domain: Material and Economic resources

Berry Street Childhood Institute, Australia	Achieve • Domain: Education and learning • Domain: Positive sense of self • Domain: Being • Domain: Age appropriate independence and competence • Domain: Building resilience Belong • Domain: Love, care and commitment • Domain: Culture and spiritual connection • Domain: Positive social relationships • Domain: Participation • Domain: Child-friendly communities • (Berry Institute, 2017, p. 23)
State of America's Children 2020	• Child population • Child poverty • Income and wealth inequality • Housing and homelessness • Child hunger and nutrition • Child health • Early childhood • Education • Child welfare • Youth justice • Gun violence (Children's Defense Fund, 2020, p. ii).

Low-income Black and Brown American children might have a better childhood, if not for misguided, harmful education reforms. Levin and Van Hoorn (2016) interviewed and observed 34 experienced early childhood teachers working in schools with large numbers of children in poverty about the impact of school reforms. The reforms led to an increase in teaching narrow academic skills and excessive testing and teaching to the test, while the time for play and child-centered learning declined. Although these reforms claim to be the best way to help low-income children of color, these teachers found they harmed children's development and learning, behavior, well-being, and attitudes toward learning and school. Many teachers shared how they were no longer able to use culturally and developmentally appropriate practices to meet the needs of the children, resulting in an increase in stress and dissatisfaction with the teaching profession. One teacher summed up her frustration when she said,

> I read articles about appropriate practice and totally agree. Then I walk into my classroom and can't do anything like what I read about. Our administrators dictate how and what we teach—lesson-by-lesson, worksheet-by-worksheet—for all children. They know nothing about ECE [early childhood education] and don't listen to us. They just want good test scores and think following the mandated curriculum is how to get them. Now that the scores aren't as good as they want (SURPRISE!), the kids and I will be punished. (Levin & Van Hoorn, 2016, p. 9)

Levin and Van Hoorn contend that proponents of these reforms have good intentions but lack formal knowledge of how children develop best. The evidence presented on the impact of these reforms makes it clear that whatever good intentions there might have been no longer matter given the disastrous outcomes. The push for universal standards and test-based accountability has ensured that many children, especially low-income children of color, are left behind and as their childhood is commodified.

Play As The Antidote To GERM!

Stop This Madness: Back to the Real Basics

Given the shameful state of childhood in the United States, it is clear that we must stop the current approach to early childhood care and education. Adding more rigorous standards and testing children nonstop does nothing to improve their cognitive, social/emotional, language, moral/spiritual, or physical development. Neoliberal reforms cannot mitigate the effects of poverty because they are purposefully blind to the reality of poverty or shift blame for poverty to the poor by way of deficit ideologies. Giving parents vouchers or opening up charter schools does nothing to alter the fundamental problems plaguing public education. At best, these measures fuel the myth of meritocracy by handpicking a small percentage of low-income, Black, and Brown youth to be deemed "winners" of the educational survival complex (Love, 2019). But as Love (2019) teaches, we must want more than for a few children to survive; we must want all children to thrive.

What does it mean for young children to thrive in school? *Failure to thrive* is a medical term that means a child does not gain weight at a rate similar to other children of the same age. However, thriving is more than just physical growth and maturation. We must consider thriving in all areas of development: physical, social, emotional, intellectual, and moral. Based on the indicators of child well-being discussed earlier, thriving is dependent on both macro and micro systems and structures. In Nordic countries, parents receive support from the government to ensure the society can make the good childhood a reality (Wagner, 2008). In Australia, the Berry Street Institute examines the good childhood in light of the strength of relationships children have in families and communities. It notes that "children thrive in nurturing environments that encourage them to explore and engage safely with the world around them, and support them to fulfill their potential" (Berry Street, 2017, p. 13). And in the United States, ensuring all children attend high-quality schools,[2] are well fed, and have a safe home, access to health care, and support to develop their full potential would allow them to succeed and provide an entryway for thriving to happen (Children's Defense Fund, 2020).

If we are to focus on thriving as the best outcome of a good childhood, then we must return to the basics. I do not mean the traditional basics that emphasized curricular knowledge in reading, writing, and arithmetic, but the basics of what we know about child development. Developmental theorists have espoused various beliefs on the mechanisms of development and the relationship between development and learning. Although they differ on stages and the role of nature versus nurture, the major theorists recognize the value of play. Through his sociocultural lens, Vygotsky viewed play as a significant contributor to cognitive development. Contemporary scholars extended Vygotsky's understanding of play to the notion of play as a leading activity (Gutiérrez et al., 2019).

A leading activity is an activity that causes the most development to occur during a particular period (Duncan & Tarulli, 2003; Gutiérrez et al., 2019). Leading activity theory posits that during infancy, the leading activity is attachment to the nuclear family. During early childhood, play becomes the leading activity. Formal schooling shifts the leading activity from play to learning, and adulthood shifts the leading activity to work (Gutiérrez et al., 2019). However, some contemporary scholars in the field of learning science view "play as a leading activity that spans the lifetime rather than an activity specific to young children" (Gutiérrez et al., 2019, p. 72). If play is the leading activity during the early childhood years (and throughout life), then it is the natural mechanism for thriving to occur.

Play: Benefits and Challenges

The universal recognition of play as a central feature of childhood (and beyond) has not led to a universal definition of play. Most early childhood experts agree that play is any self-directed activity, freely chosen by the person engaging it, without any external rules, and brings about joy or personal fulfillment (Brown, 2014; Sahlberg & Doyle, 2019). In their recent book about the necessity of play in the lives of children, Sahlberg and Doyle (2019) identify a variety of activities that include free play, guided play, play-based activities, and a humorous or playful approach utilized by a teacher. At the First International True Play Conference in Anji, China, the definition of *true play* shared with participants was "deep and uninterrupted engagement in the activity of one's own choice" (Jones, 2019a, para. 3). Taken together, through play, children retain their subjective being and their childhood is protected from commodification.

In schools, play can range from formal games with rules to unstructured time for recess. Play-based learning is often touted as an approach to teaching that includes open-ended child-directed play but includes teacher-directed activities presented as a fun game. I view play on a continuum from no play (children have no time or space to play) to true play (children have uninterrupted time to select how and what they do with open-ended materials). Teachers who promote teaching and learning through play intentionally structure the school day to include multiple opportunities for extended periods of true play.

Numerous research studies and policies that focus on a child's right to play provide ample documentation on the benefits of play. Leading professional organizations, including the American Academy of Pediatrics (Yogman et al., 2018) and the National Academy of Medicine (Kohl & Cook, 2013), issued reports on the physical, cognitive, social, and emotional benefits of play. Sahlberg and Doyle (2019) note that UNICEF working with a team of Canadian public health researchers, documented a wide range of benefits of outdoor play. As children get older, the need for recess and physical education is also well documented (Pellegrini & Bjorklund, 1997; Ramstetter et al., 2010). Frequent breaks, such as recess or physical activity, enhance children's cognitive abilities (Kibbe et al., 2011).

Although research established the benefits of play, many children's ability to engage in true play is constrained. As schools feel the pressure to raise test scores, recess and time for play are often replaced with additional academic demands or eliminated for punitive reasons. Fears regarding safety often restrict children's access to time and space for true play away from direct parental supervision. These limitations on children's ability to engage in play have led to a play deficit. Gray (2013) argues that a decrease in children's freedom to play is related to the rise of mental disorders and diagnosis. He notes that globally, leaders who pushed rote memorization to improve test scores now realize their approach produced adults who lack creativity, passion for learning, and imagination. Instead of emulating these countries, Gray (2013) argues that we should learn from their mistakes and give children more freedom to play. I posit that in addition to play providing the fertile ground for children to thrive, play can serve as an act of resistance against neoliberal reforms, an antidote to GERM.

True Play as Freedom True Play as Liberation

As I reflected on the presentations and observations at the First Annual True Play Conference, several themes emerged.[3] As Ms. Cheng reviewed the evolution of the true play[4] movement in Anji kindergartens, I noticed that her work was connected to the concept of freedom. Ms. Cheng strived to provide an environment that gave children agency over their play. Instead of providing children with materials that contained inherent functional limitations, her team introduced and designed loose parts and open-ended materials based on their observation and reflection on the children's needs in play. As the children were free to explore these materials, they began to construct elaborate and sophisticated play structures (see Figure 3.1). Thus, true play meant giving children the freedom to explore and create outside of the traditional constraints from predetermined activities and materials with limited function.

Freedom was not only limited to the children's experience but also extended to the role of the teacher. As the children expanded their play, the teachers engaged in deep observation and reflection. Instead of guiding or interfering in the children's play, the teachers were free to watch and learn. Thus, the role of the teacher shifted from providing knowledge to witnessing and documenting the children's development and learning. I noticed that the Anji kindergarten teachers mostly stayed back until a child requested their help or that the teacher felt as though their presence was needed to maintain safety. All teachers were responsible for filming children

Figure 3.1. Examples of Structures Built by Children in Anji Kindergartens.

during play. These photos and videos were used during play sharing, where children discussed their play stories (drawings of their play) as the teacher provided opportunities for children to lead whole group conversations about their play. We learned that teachers used videos and photos as a tool for staff reflections. It became apparent to me that true play freed the children to fully immerse themselves in the leading activity. And it also freed the teachers to see the children deeply engaged and brimming with potential.

Another theme that emerged from the conference presentations and observations at Anji kindergartens was liberation. Professor Feng Xiaoxia from Beijing Normal University shared how, as the teachers witnessed deep learning, they were no longer constrained by an image of the child that negated their potential for deep learning. As the opportunity to engage in true play freed the child, it also liberated both the teacher and the children. The teacher was liberated from the traditional deficit views of young children and free to see themselves as a co-learner with the children. The children were liberated from environments that focused on survival and were free to thrive and teach their teacher how they learned through play. The freedom inherent in play liberated both the teacher and the child and becomes our best option for protecting childhood from GERM.

Resisting GERM With A Play Pedagogy

Play is essential for healthy child development and has the power to ensure that school is a place where children thrive. Under GERM, education becomes the epitome of what Freire (2000) described as the banking concept of education, whereby teachers make knowledge deposits into children who become depositories. In this system, children are expected to survive. Surviving means earning the required measures of success, that is, a high school diploma and decent test scores, and may even include the ability to feel prepared for the future. But thriving is not possible in an education system dominated by GERM. Thriving requires a child-centered, engaging curriculum and an environment centered on the needs and interests of the child. To ensure the early years are a space for thriving, early childhood teachers can resist GERM. And they can enact a play pedagogy that allows children to experience an education that is more liberating, social justice–oriented, antiracist, and critical (Solo & Swadener, 2015).

Pedagogy is the approach one takes to the task of educating someone else. Some pedagogies are influenced by one's prevailing beliefs about the best method for teaching and learning, such as a constructivist pedagogy (Richardson, 2003), or come from an ideology such as feminist pedagogy (Shrewsbury, 1987) or liberatory pedagogy (Bray, 2004). A play pedagogy builds on the belief that play is the primary way children learn and should be the principal activity utilized in the classroom. Typically, when play is incorporated in early childhood settings, it is often used as a break from learning. Children can play for 30 to 45 minutes at centers or stations, such as blocks or dramatic play, with materials limited to the function of that center. Other times, play becomes synonymous with recess or what children do during recess. A play pedagogy centers children's opportunity to engage in play as the primary approach to teaching and learning.

A play pedagogy expands the curriculum and connects it to learning that is personal and meaningful. Instead of focusing on discrete bits of knowledge and measurable skills, a pedagogy of play allows children to engage in inquiry and problem-solving, with opportunities to reinforce literacy, math, science, social studies, and art. Instead of expecting children to learn these academic subjects in isolation at particular times of the day, they become intertwined and deeply embedded in the natural work of children as they explore, create, reflect, and build. A play pedagogy is not driven by standards or packaged curriculums that dictate what children should learn and should do by a specific time. The interests and desires of the child determine what the child will learn and can do.

If children are not required to memorize facts and perform for their teachers, then standardized assessments become obsolete. A play pedagogy invites authentic assessments that take place in natural settings, focus on what children can do, and are guided by the teacher's observation of the children. Standardized assessments that purport to be objective measures of a student's capabilities are more likely to measure parental income and resources available to children (Ravitch, 2013). Assessment of young children should not strive for objectivity that sees the child devoid of their family culture, language diversity, and modes of thinking. Instead, teachers should document children's capabilities through observation and reflection. Hence, a play pedagogy shifts the role of the teacher and the purpose of assessment, making teaching and learning a process where the whole child can develop and thrive.

Given the poor statistics of child well-being in the United States, we know that many children suffer from trauma, toxic stress, and adverse childhood experiences. Research has found a link between early childhood adversity and an increase in negative outcomes, including health-related illnesses (Bethell et al., 2014), behavioral problems in school (Hunt et al., 2017), high school graduation (Giovanelli et al., 2015), and language development in kindergarten (Jimenez et al., 2015). Despite recognizing that many children experience high levels of trauma and toxic stress, the research is clear that resilience is the key to mitigating the impact on adult health (Bellis, 2017).

We might not be able to end childhood poverty or make sure every child has a safe home and health care without a commitment from our government and realignment of our values. Still, we can help children develop the resilience they need to thrive despite the disadvantages they face. Unlike the neoliberal concept of grit that implies the measuring and commodification of one's ability to survive challenges, resilience is not something you measure but instead is something you nourish. We know play builds resilience and can be therapeutic for children experiencing adversity. As today's children live through a global pandemic, they will need unlimited opportunities for imaginative play to process their feelings and experience. Folostina et al. (2015) studied the impact of utilizing play and drama sessions with children exhibiting negative behaviors in response to high levels of trauma and stress. They found that the use of creative work sessions led to a decrease in disruptive behaviors and an increase in confidence. When teachers enact a play pedagogy, they give children the tools they need to enhance their self-efficacy, self-esteem, sense of agency, and self-regulation.

A Global True Play Revolution: My Vision For The Future

Although GERM continues to spread, all is not lost. Through our collective advocacy, we have made others aware of the damage these reforms inflict on young children. We have formed alliances with parents, teachers, and community members who know that childhood needs protection. And most important, educators have a low-cost method we can implement in our classrooms that will resist the GERM infestation, free children and their teachers, liberate early childhood education, and promote thriving and resilience. The teachers in Anji, China, are leading the global true play revolution, and they are joined by educators around the world who believe in the power of play. If we can use our role as teachers of young children to resist neoliberal reforms and insist on using a play pedagogy, perhaps we can let the children save us from our failures.

As I continue developing and mentoring early childhood teachers, I dream of witnessing the global true play revolution in action. I imagine going into spaces full of young children actively engaged in a variety of tasks. I can see them smiling at a new discovery, thinking hard about a complex problem, and working together to accomplish a task. Their teachers watch closely and document their learning. They are trusted to support and guide student's learning through play. Together they reflect, assess, plan, and prepare for another day of pursuing their interests. Their parents are pleased by their enthusiasm for school and know that they are learning so much from the stories they share. Society values learning guided by a child's ability to ask and answer essential questions that goes far beyond memorizing facts and performing discrete disconnected skills. As they get older their right to play continues to guide their educational experience. Each school year they embark on in-depth projects that allow for deep exploration into topics worthy of study in ways that reinforce the learner's curiosity and drive. Their pursuit of knowledge is valued more than how many things they learn. They thrive in an environment that embraces their full humanity. This vision for the future reminds me that early childhood education designed to protect childhood through a pedagogy of play can indeed save the world.

Notes

1. Scholars are questioning whether the achievement gap is a racist idea. See Kendi (2016).
2. Although not defined, the paradox is that high-quality schools are often those with the highest test scores.
3. I first wrote about these themes in my blog *What is the Power of True Play? Play as Freedom, Play as Liberation* published on September 27, 2019; see https://dey.org/what-is-the-power-of-true-play-play-as-freedom-play-as-liberation/.
4. For a fuller description of true play see my blog *What is True Play?* published on May 23, 2019; see https://dey.org/what-is-true-play/.

References

Bassok, D., Latham, S., & Rorem, A. (2016). Is kindergarten the new first grade? *AERA Open*. https://doi.org/10.1177/2332858415616358

Bellis, M.A., Hardcastle, K., Ford, K., Hughes, K., Ashton, K., Quigg, Z., & Butler, N. (2017). Does continuous trusted adult support in childhood impact life-course resilience against adverse childhood experiences—a retrospective study on adult health-harming behaviours and mental well-being. *BMC Psychiatry, 17*, Article 110. doi:10.1186/s12888-017-1260-z

Berry Street. (2017). *What makes a good childhood?* Berry Street Childhood Institute. https://learning.berrystreet.org.au/resources/what-makes-good-childhood

Bethell, C. D., Newacheck, P., Hawes, E., & Halfon, N. (2014). Adverse childhood experiences: Assessing the impact on health and school engagement and the mitigating role of resilience. *Health Affairs, 33*(12), 2106–2115. http://dx.doi.org/10.1377/hlthaff.2014.0914

Bray, P. M. (2004). Young women majoring in mathematics and elementary education: A perspective on enacting liberatory pedagogy. *Equity & Excellence in Education, 37*(1),44–54. https://doi.org/10.1080/10665680490422098

Brown, F. (2014). *Play & playwork: 101 stories of children playing.* Open Hill Press.

Children's Defense Fund. (2020). *The state of America's children 2020.*

Duncan, R. M., & Tarulli, D. (2003) Play as the leading activity of the preschool period: Insights from Vygotsky, Leont'ev, and Bakhtin. *Early Education & Development, 14*(3), 271–292. doi:10.1207/s15566935eed1403_2

FairTest. (2019, May). *Graduation test update: States that Recently eliminated or scaled back high school exit exams* (Updated MAY 2019). https://www.fairtest.org/graduation-test-update-states-recently-eliminated

Freire, P. (2000). *Pedagogy of the oppressed* (30th anniversary ed.). Continuum.

Folostina, R., Tudorache, L., Michel, T., Erzebet, B., Agheana, V., & Hocagolu, H. (2105). Using play and drama in developing resilience in children at risk. *Procedia—Social and Behavioral Sciences, 197*(1), 2362–2368. doi:10.1016/j.sbspro.2015.07.283

Giovanelli, A., Reynolds, A. J., Mondi, C.F., & Ou, S. (2016). Adverse childhood experiences and adult well-being in a low-income, urban cohort. *Pediatrics, 137*(4), Article e20154016.

Gray, P. (2013, September 18). *The play-deficit.* https://aeon.co/essays/children-today-are-suffering-a-severe-deficit-of-play

Gutiérrez, K. D., Higgs, J., Lizárraga, J. R., & Rivero, E. (2019). Learning as movement in social design-based experiments: Play as a leading activity. *Human Development, 62*(1–2), 66–82. doi:10.1159/000496239

Hatch, J. A. (2002). Accountability shovedown: Resisting the standards movement in early childhood education. *Phi Delta Kappan, 83*(6), 457–462. doi: 10.1177/003172170208300611

Hunt, T. K. A., Berger, L. M., & Slack, K. S. (2017). Adverse childhood experiences and behavioral problems in middle childhood. *Child Abuse & Neglect, 67*, 391–402. doi:10.1016/j.chiabu.2016.11.005

Jimenez, M. E., Wade, R., Lin, Y., Morrow, L. M., & Reichman, N. E. (2015). Adverse experiences in early childhood and kindergarten outcomes. *Pediatrics, 137*(2), Article e20151839.

Jones, D. (2019a, May 24). *What is true play?* Defending the Early Years. https://dey.org/what-is-true-play/

Jones, D. (2019b, June 18). *How a true play revolution can protect childhood.* Defending the Early Years. https://dey.org/how-a-true-play-revolution-can-protect-childhood/

Kendi, I. X. (2016, October 20). *Why the academic achievement gap is a racist idea.* Black Perspectives. https://www.aaihs.org/why-the-academic-achievement-gap-is-a-racist-idea/

Kibbe, D. L., Hackett, J., Hurley, M., McFarland, A., Godburn Schubert, L., Shultz, A., & Harris, S. (2011). Ten years of TAKE 10!: Integrating physical activity with academic concepts in elementary school classrooms. *Preventive Medicine, 53*(Suppl. 1), S42–S50. https://doi.org/10.1016/j.ypmed.2011.01.025

Kohl III, H. W., & Cook, H. D. (Eds.). (2013). *Educating the student body: Taking physical activity and physical education to school.* The National Academies Press, Institute of Medicine.

Levin, D. E., & Van Hoorn, J. L. (2016). *Teachers speak out: How school reforms are failing low-income young children.* Defending the Early Years. https://dey.org/publication/defending-the-early-years-releases-its-latest-report-teachers-speak-out-how-school-reforms-are-failing-low-income-young-children/

Love, B. L. (2019). *We want to do more than survive: Abolitionist teaching and the pursuit of educational freedom.* Beacon Press.

Miller, E., & Almon, J. (2009). *Crisis in the kindergarten: Why children need to play in school.* Alliance for Childhood.

Nichols, S. L., & Berliner, D. C. (2007). *Collateral damage: How high-stakes testing corrupts America's schools.* Harvard Education Press.

Pellegrini, A. D., & Bjorklund, D. F. (1997). The role of recess in children's cognitive performance. *Educational Psychologist, 32*(1), 35–40. http://dx.doi.org/10.1207/s15326985ep3201_3

Ramstetter, C. L., Murray, R., & Garner, A.S. (2010). The crucial role of recess in schools. *Journal of School Health, 80*(11), 517–526.

Ravitch, D. (2013). *Reign of error: The hoax of the privatization movement and the danger to America's public schools.* Alfred A. Knopf.

Repko-Erwin, M. E. (2017). Was kindergarten left behind? Examining US kindergarten as the new first-grade in the wake of No Child Left Behind. *Global Education Review, 4*(2), 58–74.

Richardson, V. (2004). Constructivist pedagogy. *Teachers College Record, 105*(9), 1623–1640.

Sahlberg, P., & Doyle, W. (2019). *Let the children play: How more play will save our schools and help children thrive.* Oxford University Press.

Shrewsbury, C. M. (1987). What is feminist pedagogy? *Women's Studies Quarterly, 15*(3/4), 6–14.

Soto, L. D., & Swadener, B. B. (2002). Toward liberatory early childhood theory, research, and praxis: Decolonizing a field. *Contemporary Issues in Early Childhood, 3*(1), 38–66.

Stearns, P. N. (2015). History of childhood. In J. M. Rey (Ed.), *IACAPAP e-textbook of child and adolescent mental health* (Chapter J.9, 1–32). International Association for Child and Adolescent Psychiatry and Allied Professionals.

Vygotsky, L. S. (1967/2016). Play and its role in the mental development of the child (N. Veresov & M. Barrs, Trans.). *International Research in Early Childhood Education, 7*(2), 3–25. (Original work published in 1967).

Wagner, J. T. (2008). The good childhood: Nordic ideals and educational practice. *International Journal of Educational Research, 47*(5), 265–269. doi:10.1016/j.ijer.2008.12.005

Wasmuth, H., & Nitecki, E. (2017). Global early childhood policies: The impact of the global education reform movement and possibilities for reconceptualization. *Global Education Review, 4*(2), 1–17.

Yogman, M., Garner, A., Hutchinson, J., Hirsh-Pasek, K., & Golinkoff, R. M. (2018). The power of play: A pediatric role in enhancing development in young children. *Pediatrics, 142*(3), e20182058.

Chapter Four

HOW SCHOOLS REINFORCE SOCIALLY CONSTRUCTED NOTIONS OF "SMARTNESS" AND HOW WE CAN SUBVERT THEM THROUGH TRUST

by T. Jameson Brewer & Scott T. Grubbs

As other chapters in this volume explore theoretical and practical implications of commodification across the educational landscape and provide possible solutions moving forward, the aim of this chapter is to describe how educational policy has enabled the commodification of teaching and learning over time, suggest what purposes commodification serves, and, perhaps, reimagine what better policy could facilitate across our nation's schools.

The majority of contemporary educational policies find their ideological origins in *A Nation at Risk* (1983), published during the Reagan administration, setting the tone for every subsequent administration's understanding of education. The report presents a context for commodification, competition, and individualism. In the assumptions and proposals of *A Nation at Risk*, rather than being understood as a public or common good, schooling is a service offered in a market to consumers, parents and students. School's service provides the opportunity for students to accumulate a type of currency in the form of records of academic performance for the purpose of purchasing credentials, namely, degrees (Labaree, 1988, 1997a, 1997b; Maier, 2012). These credentials become currency in the subsequent markets in our lives, the domestic and global marketplace of employment and actual money (Brewer & Potterton, 2020).

The somewhat ludicrous central argument of *A Nation at Risk* was that U.S. public schools had failed. Accepting schools and teachers as failed facilitated a policy environment ripe for reform. As with any solution, the report and its attendant recommendations must purport to address a problem. If public schools actually had failed as democratic institutions funded collectively to serve the common good, throwing more money into them and continuing to operate schooling under the same conceptions would have made little sense (Greene et al., 2005; Walberg & Bast, 2003). What was needed, the reformers claimed, was a shifting of the overt understandings of schooling away from conceptions of the common good to a more individualistic, marketized approach in which consumers (e.g., parents and students) would be able to hold schools accountable for their perceived shortfalls and, equally, allow policy makers to "begin" to hold schools accountable for their receipt of public dollars. For policy makers, what became more necessary was a fast metric by which to classify schools, teachers, and students as successes or failures: standardized testing. While quantifiable metrics and commensuration efforts are not exclusive to education (Muller, 2018), they drive the majority of educational policies and contemporary pedagogical practices, which is unique within matters of public policy. School is the only institution governed by standardized testing.

Because it has long been known that academic achievement is almost entirely informed by out-of-school factors and family socioeconomic status (Bowles & Gintis, 1976; Grusky, 2008; Jencks & Phillips, 1998; Jencks et al., 1972; Kozol, 1991; Massey, 2007; Massey & Denton, 1993), the great value placed on high-stakes assessments and the test scores they produce signaled a commitment on the part of the nation's policy makers to a distorted and inequitable concept of merit in which academic achievement and its rewards are limited to a privileged minority while children from marginalized groups are pushed further toward the educational and economic brink. In the current policy landscape, merit is interpreted as academic performance, measured strictly by test scores. All things being equal, this might be reasonable, but most things are not equal. Funding, community resources, and cultural and linguistic distances from the test—just about every element of real life for students and teachers—are neither standard nor equivalent. As a result, the intended outcomes on which policy actions are based have little connection to merit. Instead, they end up reinforcing existing social and economic gaps. By putting test scores at the center of policy and funding, we have created a false sense of merit that, in effect, justifies the societal inequalities of race and class that perpetuate beyond the classroom (Markovits, 2019).

In what follows, we explore what constitutes "smartness," which, in this skewed frame, is supposed to be the central commodity determining merit. Understanding smartness as a commodity is both cause and product of the policy orientation in which education is seen as an individualistic good. At the same time, the interpretation of merit as smartness provides cover for those who want to believe that systemic inequalities in schools and society are the fault of those who suffer from them.

Smartness As Commodity

Notions of smartness are informed through the context within which an ideology is created, especially the ends that such notions serve. As contexts shift within a society, so do the criteria that compose smartness and the value placed on such characteristics by the decision-makers in that society. For example, what constituted smartness in colonial America is quite different from what constitutes smartness in the modern United States. Historians laud the ingenuity and smartness of early Mesopotamians, who developed early farming and storage practices, yet that type of pragmatic knowledge is hardly celebrated in today's modern society. Rather than defining smartness as the possession of pragmatic knowledge and skills, today's definition of smartness, we argue, is limited to standardized knowledge that is typically learned and assessed in rote methods. Collectively, we look to our nation's schools to inculcate "skills" that prepare students for future work. Along the way, schools purport to predict a student's future abilities by assigning value in the form of grades and test scores as an indication of an individual's smartness. In turn, schools in the United States have dramatically shaped our societies' definition of smartness, made it easier to demarcate who is smart and who is not along those myopic lines, and, most interestingly, aligned daily practices to ensure that the goal of the production of smartness is at the forefront of activities and focus. The demarcation of who is smart and who is not provides the opportunity to justify socioeconomic inequalities. And, in the extreme, White supremacists such as Herrnstein and Murray (1994) have used conceptions of smartness as measured by IQ tests to understand and justify racial economic gaps. Moreover,

> test-based accountability, in practice, is a rationale for the divestment of [from] public schools—a narrative for the withdrawal of funds to schools that don't demonstrate upward moving scores—and a narrowing of the activities of schooling, to what can be measurable. (Carini, 2001, as cited in Tuck, 2012, p. 43)

Up to this point, we have likened the concept of smartness to currency, a commodity, and policy. But above all, smartness, as it appears in the U.S. education system, is a tool, specifically one that has been weaponized by a variety of stakeholders, including policy makers, business and industrial leaders, and—perhaps ironically—a significant number of educators, who have by extension convinced students and parents that test-derived smartness is the only path to professional success and personal happiness. Hatt's (2012) description of smartness further underscores the ways in which schools reinforce dominant perceptions of smartness to the benefit of some and the detriment of many. In describing smartness as "more verb than noun," Hatt suggests that "smartness or implicit intelligence is something done to others as social positioning" (2012, p. 439). In a real sense, Hatt's conceptualization of smartness is very much reminiscent of a weapon that inflicts considerable harm on its intended victims through the imposition of high-stakes hierarchies that grant present and future status and success based on metrics that are at once quantitative and arbitrary. Worse, the multiple harms that smartness inflicts on the students in the nation's schools have been embraced and enshrined in virtually every major national educational reform initiative from George H. W. Bush's Goals 2000 to the current Every Student Succeeds Act (ESSA). Through social positioning built on discriminatory views of what constitutes smartness, how smartness is determined, who is considered smart, and why it matters, policy makers and others charged with the education and welfare of our students not only built a formidable weapon but also turned it on our children and pulled the trigger.

What follows here is an examination of the literature surrounding schooling practices that reinforce the socially constructed notion of smartness and suggestions on how educators can counter the deleterious practices of smartness that undermine real educative experiences for students. As former K–12 teachers ourselves, we recognize the pressing need to address the narrowing of the meaning of education to formalized mandates of schooling while also recognizing the need for pragmatic solutions.

On How We Define The Creation of "Smartness"

Schools in the United States are often characterized as the "great equalizer" (Brewer & Myers, 2015). As such, schools are seen as the mechanism that renders the socioeconomic status of students irrelevant, at least within the confines of its classrooms. In this view, all students have the same opportunity to apply smartness that will be manifested in high grades and later cashed in for college admission and/or good well-paying jobs. Therefore, it seems important to understand how schools define smartness and the processes by which this ideology is conveyed and practiced within our nation's schools.

At present, our schools operate in such a way as to consider merit, and the meritocracy that follows, as a commonsensical reality for both how schools ought to function and how the world interacts. This premise is founded on Michael Young's assertion that an "individuals' social status and wealth would be based entirely on their own deserved merits, [where merit is defined] as the product of intelligence and effort" (Korp, 2011, p. 22). Education policy and schools operate under the assumption that the underlying contributor to success (defined by good grades while in school and by high salaries when employed as an adult) is informed by an individual's intelligence and effort—or "smartness." Inasmuch as a student works hard, she will develop her smartness, display increased merit, and, ultimately, reap the benefits of higher social status and wealth.

However, some have suggested that schools are not the great equalizer; rather, schools serve as the means by which socioeconomic inequalities are perpetuated under the guise of meritocracy (Anyon, 1980, 1997; Bowles & Gintis, 1976; McLaren, 2011), and Hatt (2012) posits that smartness, as a verb, is the process by which individuals are positioned within the social stratification. In this view, the demarcation of smartness becomes the means by which socioeconomic stratification becomes justified. What is portrayed in the usual ideology as an active means to deserved achievement is far more often a foregone conclusion that maintains and rationalizes existing privilege. As students are indoctrinated into believing the school's definition of smartness and the belief that their socioeconomic status is determined by merit, they are likely to accept their fate as the result of their own doing (Sennett & Cobb, 1973). Moreover, the shifting of the onus to achieve along such narrow understandings of schooling affords policy makers the opportunity to ignore larger societal ills. For example, generational poverty is to be understood not as a systemic societal failure but as an artifact of cultural deficits and failures of individuals.

Increasingly, schools define intelligence as measured by student performance on standardized exams (Sacks, 1999) despite serious challenges to the validity of tests to measure student learning (Baker, 2011; Glass, 2008; Ravitch, 2010, 2013). Moreover, there has been an incessant push to link teacher salaries—or bonuses—to the production of smartness as assessed via testing (Berlak, 2011; Chamberlin et al., 2002; Finnigan, 2008; Protsik, 1995; Springer et al., 2010), which has caused some instances of documented cheating (Brumback, 2013; Knoester, 2012) and can lead to a breakdown in professional collaboration (Brewer et al., 2015). Yet, despite the cultural differences in how smartness is defined, the perceived meritocracy that we live in labels a particular kind of smartness as valuable social capital. This replaces a culturally relevant curriculum (Delpit, 2009, 2012) and reduces learning to a practice of certainty and "best practices" that seek to produce smartness while simultaneously engaging in cultural eugenics (Horn, 2011) and represents a new iteration of colonialism (Tuck, 2012).

School Practices That Reinforce Notions of Smartness

Individual schools, and school districts at large, are increasingly held accountable to the ends that they do, or do not, raise student test scores—again, a taken-for-granted indicator of student smartness. In fact, rating entire states based on their perceived ability to raise student test scores—as a measure of smartness—has become a popular practice by policy-oriented organizations such as the American Legislative Exchange Council (Ladner & Myslinski, 2013) and is cited often by policy makers at the local, state, and federal levels as "evidence" of the need to reform schools, often through privatization. In response to this practice, many districts have instituted incentive and punitive structures to encourage schools and teachers to raise test scores. This, in turn, becomes a reflection of the level of smartness that a student can have conferred upon them if they attend such a school (assuming, of course, that schools provide an equal opportunity for all students—which they do not). On the contrary, schools that fail to increase scores are to be subjected to competition in an effort to promote better practices that elicit better results and more evidence, as it were, of smartness.

Stemming from our societal belief in meritocracy, we have established the means by which we perpetuate a stratified economy. As the income gap continues to grow inexorably here in the United States and resources are evermore confined, there exists the need to ensure that access to resources be limited in such a way as to maintain the status quo. Our nation's ideological commitment to meritocracy and capitalism informs the political economy that is a real wage and wealth gap. This ideology and lived reality, in turn, find root and perpetuation in our schools through the use of class and diploma tracking as a substitute proxy for the commodity of learning. The practice of sorting students into predetermined tracks that inform future work opportunities assumes that (a) the main purpose of schooling is to prepare students for jobs (Bills, 2004), (b) there is a natural bell curve of innate abilities (Herrnstein & Murray, 1994), and (c) that the acquisition of smartness be bounded by different curriculums for different students, chosen by the consumer (Hatfield & Malkus, 2017). Moreover, as smartness is defined as the capital by which individuals are rewarded with good jobs, education shifts further away from a conception of what is best for the public good and closer to a conception of education as an individual right or individual good. This practice "has reshaped education into a commodity for the purposes of status attainment and has elevated the pursuit of credentials over the acquisition of knowledge" (Labaree, 1997b, p. 39).

Because of the interpretation of schooling as the mechanism for the production of smartness and the dramatic increase in demands for teacher accountability, many teachers have resorted to teaching to the test or, as was the case in the Atlanta Public Schools, cheating on the tests. In effect, many teachers employ such practices due to the increased pressure to raise student test scores to maintain their job as a teacher, to keep their school off the No Child Left Behind (NCLB) "endangered species" list so prevalent in educational reform policies, such as NCLB, Race to the Top (RTTT), and the ESSA, or to maintain or increase their salary via merit pay. To date, Atlanta Public Schools was the site of the largest school cheating scandal in U.S. history. To perpetuate a mirage of successful yearly gains and to receive a monetary bonus, teachers throughout the district voluntarily or involuntarily gave students answers during tests or erased wrong answers and replaced them with correct ones at a later date. Such practices are indicative of the extent to which some districts will go to maintain an image of producing smartness. These practices—teaching to the test or cheating on the test—manifest themselves through school rating systems, media coverage, and individual student transcripts as artifacts of smartness (Hatt, 2012, p. 447). And, as pointed out by Hatt (2012), students use these artifacts of smartness "as a tool of social positioning" (p. 455). In sum, this is what we know:

1. Conceptions of smartness, as a metric associated with a student's ability and "hard work" to learn, is elevated as the capital, or currency, in the neoliberal and neo-essentialist paradigm to obtain status (both as a student and as a future citizen).
2. Knowledge outside of the prescribed standardized curriculum is understood as not useful, a waste of time (think a student doodling in a notebook), and unworthy of exploration
3. Given the rise of quantification (Muller, 2018) under the past few federal policies (e.g., NCLB, RTTT, ESSA), those academic subjects that are not as easily quantifiable for the purpose of measuring and comparing (e.g., social studies, music, art, etc.) are forced to take a back seat to mathematics and literacy metrics. While this falls in line with Point 2, it also reinforces a narrowing of the curriculum away from the humanities, this approach

understands learning as a direct pathway to quantifiable employment rather than the self-actualization of the student as fully human.

4. Schools become the sites in which this conception of a specific type of "smartness" as a commodity is reinforced and the myth of meritocracy is reified. Those students who are privileged with relative affluence and racial privilege in society will be able to leverage their family's resources and the unequal distribution of school funding—note, schools that dominantly serve White students receive $23 billion in *additional* funding each year that schools that serve Black and Brown students do not receive (EdBuild, 2019)—to appear "smarter" in this game despite the deck being stacked in their favor.

With this understanding, we can see how students who are raised up to believe that their achievement of smartness is an artifact of their self-worth thus entitling them to the spoils of merit and how socioeconomic inequality is largely tolerated.

COVID-19: When Smartness "Trumped" Life Itself

An example of our nation's commitment to understanding smartness as measurable, quantified, learning and its currency as a commodity have been on full display during the COVID-19 pandemic. Scientific evidence suggested that social distancing measures—including school closures—potentially contributed to the reduction of COVID-19 incidence and spread (Auger et al., 2020; Head et al., 2020). And, if schools were to reopen, extraordinary precautions, including reduced class sizes, hybridization, or complete virtual instruction would need to be taken to mitigate infections among students, faculty, and staff (Head et al., 2020). Yet the manner in which many policy makers responded to efforts to reopen schools following what was a nationwide shuttering of schools and then a normal summer break illustrated a perceived fear of students "falling behind" academically. Quite often, this perceived learning deficit was measured in some quantifiable metric of *x* months of learning. Additionally, the impetus for reopening schools took an ethical turn, with advocates arguing that keeping students at home caused far greater social, emotional, and cognitive developmental harms than the physical risks associated with reentering classrooms—particularly for marginalized students (Silverman et al., 2020).

Academic, ethical, and other concerns regarding school closures found full-throated support from President Trump, education secretary DeVos, and other members of the Trump administration, all of whom strongly advocated for the immediate reopening of the nation's school districts. Following the lead of President Trump, many governors and local school boards—particularly in the South—championed full-scale openings of K–12 schools and universities in opposition to the medical and scientific consensus that such actions would contribute to the already-growing rise in the spread of a deadly virus. Ironically, President Trump's push for wholesale school reopenings contradicted the safety criteria outlined in his administration's "Opening America Again" initiative (Courtemanche et al., 2020) and was indicative of his desire to prioritize educational commoditization and related political gain over the lives of children and those who work to educate them.

Compounding matters, school reopenings frequently occurred with little to no legitimate efforts to mitigate the spread of the virus. For example, while many school districts "recommended" or "suggested" mask wearing, few made face coverings compulsory. And while many districts suggested that they would implement mitigation efforts as best as possible, most also acknowledged that such efforts would not be possible on school buses—likely nullifying other in-school efforts anyway. What was at stake here was not necessarily the academic achievement of students—although that was used as the rationale. Beneath the policy makers' narratives surrounding the need for students to return to school-based learning environments were economic and political exigencies generated by the ongoing economic depression and the specter of the loss of football and its attendant revenue. For the economic and political status quo antebellum to be maintained, however, the public must remain convinced that the cause célèbre surrounding school openings was and remains, despite the façade, the academic achievement of students. If students were unable to attend schools in person, according to the logic, then students would fall behind academically, and students who are already at risk of lower academic achievement would, in turn, be hurt even worse. Student and teacher health and lives could not compare to the importance of the perceived threat of students falling behind on test scores. The commodification of schooling became more important than life itself.

Implications And Suggestions For Change

In the current environment, political, economic, and social forces militate schools toward a narrow and toxic conceptualization of smartness as a commodity. It would be understandable that those truly concerned about the education of our youth might view the current situation as hopeless. As Tyack and Cuban (1995) noted, schools have historically been resistant to change, and they appear to be even more so in the never-ending era of testing and accountability. In a speech to New York City teachers in October 1963 that was later published in *The Saturday Review*, writer and social critic James Baldwin stated,

> The purpose of education, finally, is to create in a person the ability to look at the world for himself, to make his own decisions, to say to himself this is black or this is white, to decide for himself whether there is a God in heaven or not. To ask questions of the universe, and then learn to live with those questions, is the way he achieves his own identity. But no society is really anxious to have that kind of person around.

> What societies want really, ideally, want is a citizenry which will simply obey the rules of society. (p. 44)

Given Baldwin's comments, it may appear that the challenges posed by the way in which school stakeholders damage students under the guise of smartness as a commodity may seem insurmountable, the problems intractable, and the harms inevitable. Indeed, the current educational climate in which smartness is determined by how well students can conform to schooling that suppresses intellectual curiosity and wonder while encouraging the development of people who are submissive and collectively ignorant of the world and their place in it as critical participants seems to reflect Baldwin's still all-too-relevant observation that "we are living through a very dangerous time" (1963, p. 42).

Rather than despair for a system that seems to have little inclination or capacity to change, however, those who care about the fate of the children in America's schools should heed Freire's (2004) admonition, "I would consider myself more than sad, desolate, and finding no meaning for my presence in the world, if compelling and indestructible reasons were to convince me that that human existence unfolds within the domain of predetermination" (p. 58). If education is truly meant to liberate by enabling all students to reach their potential, then policy makers and educators would do well to reject the hierarchical predetermination imposed by assessment-driven conceptualizations of smartness. Arguably, to accept that the current educational system is destined to sort children according to artificial conceptualizations of smartness—as dictated by economic and political priorities and expressed through inauthentic measures such as the high-stakes standardized testing policies so prevalent in our nation's public schools—represents a professional and moral failure on the part of those dedicated to the erstwhile development and protection of the children whom they claim to teach. Perhaps, ironically, the failure to take disruptive action to end the labeling, sorting, and subsequent judging of students based on perceptions of smartness traps all involved in a reproductive cycle that oppresses both educators and students, reinforces class- and race-based educational tropes, and denies the democratic potential of public education. Thus, those who care about our youth and the education they receive are duty bound to take action because they have a moral and professional duty to do so. The failure to act is tantamount to not only a betrayal of students but also a betrayal of the profession and the larger society.

Despite the frustrations associated with working in a political and economic climate that often makes them feel powerless and marginalized professionally (Markow et al., 2013; Markow & Pieters, 2012), educators—particularly teachers—still maintain the power to disrupt schooling practices that discriminate and harm students. As Ayers (2004) noted, teachers can make a significant contribution to disrupting harmful schooling paradigms through their ability to create environments that foster true education by giving both students and teachers alike the ability to "discern, critique, and rebuild to everyone's advantage" (p. 70). It is important to note Ayer's use of the term *everyone* in describing a supportive educational environment. In Ayer's vision, the chance to "discern, critique, and rebuild" is not restricted to those students whom the teacher labels "smart" or "gifted" or "a good student."

The truly educational environment exists for all students to develop according to their individual talents, interests, and experiences as well as the capacity to understand this in alignment with the broader public good. When teachers build environments where students feel challenged, are encouraged to question, to disagree, to disrupt, to reconceptualize . . . to learn (Ayers, 2004) while feeling valued and accepted for who they are and the experiences they bring with them as part of their identities, then the classroom becomes a dynamic, fluid space far removed from the dehumanizing assembly lines that our schools have become. Instead, meanings are forged, altered, destroyed, and reborn. Discourse forms and informs. Ideas take flight, fall to the earth, and are reborn with respect and dignity. All of this in an atmosphere in which all feel safe, respected, and treated with dignity. If education is, to quote Ayers, "often messy, rough, unpredictable, and inconsistent" (2004, p. 81), then surely educators must create environments and contexts that allow for the educational process to unfold—even if that environment and conception of education run counter to political and economic interpretations of schooling. Moreover, they must create such spaces in ways that respect the "smartness" of all their students in less myopic and more holistic ways. Educators who succeed in this endeavor are instrumental in building up people who can think critically, be creative, challenge assumptions, come to realize their relationship to the larger world, and are able to change those relationships for the betterment of themselves and the larger society—characteristics that are not readily measured as metrics or quantifiable for comparison. Ironically, not only are these capacities the very same ones advocated for by "disruptive" critics such as Baldwin, Tuck, Freire, and Ayers, but they are also considered to be necessary skills in such modern curriculum policies as the Common Core Standards and the Partnership for 21st Century Skills (BattelleforKids, 2019). However, in the current school contexts, whereby only those with privileged statuses have any hope to access such educational environments, the likelihood that students will enter the post-scholastic world with these necessary abilities appears increasingly problematic.

Central to the idea of disrupting current toxic educational policies and practices is the idea of trust. Trust, to be sure, is not a necessary characteristic of a meritocracy, nor can it be commoditized into a utility for capitalism. Smartness as a verb, in this way, becomes the indicator for the boundaries of our hierarchical social transactions. It is also a means by which the privileged manipulate those boundaries for their personal or class-based gain. Smartness becomes the tool by which beneficiaries rationalize, reject, or simply ignore the adverse impacts that their words and deeds have on those who are less fortunate, less "smart." Put bluntly, smartness is how the privileged "get away" with whatever they desire to do. Conversely, educators and the students they teach must feel a genuine trust if they are to struggle with difficult questions, controversial ideas, and challenge ideas about the world that have become so accepted as to seem almost inviolate. Trust is an essential component in the risk-taking, and the willingness to fail is an integral part of the educational process. It is a critical component of the moral and ethical responsibilities that educators have toward those they teach, and the cooperative spirit trust engenders is a vital element of any healthy community (Strike, 2007). Indeed, it would not be difficult to argue that, without trust, truly democratic education cannot exist.

Yet, too often, schools and classrooms demonstrate many of the characteristics of low-trust institutions outlined by Combs and colleagues (2013). In such environments, the motivation of the organization's stakeholders is constantly questioned and regarded with cynicism and suspicion. Additionally, organization members appear passive, uninvolved, and do the minimal amount of work required. In low-trust organizations, leaders focus on issues of minimal importance while other members adopt a "bunker mentality" because they do not feel emotionally secure. Finally, as a result of a lack of trust, members do not share ideas with each other, and there is little opportunity for openness in communication.

Unfortunately, it is relatively easy to see how these dispositions manifest themselves in our schools. In schools that emphasize "getting the right answer" and "improving test scores" over genuine education, students are subsequently divided based on how well they conform to standards and perform on assessments. Such students are often rewarded, while those who struggle are often marginalized and labeled with labels that reflect deficits. Ironically, these are the students who are denied access to the resources and opportunities that might help them perform better within the system. Instead, those students who already benefit from the status quo are the recipients of the wherewithal to become even more successful, leaving the marginalized behind (Wink, 2005). Not surprisingly, these students build affective barriers to both subject and teachers, causing the learning process to shut down. Often doing less than the minimum level of work that the schools find acceptable, these students become increasingly vulnerable to dropping out of a schooling system that they find irrelevant (Tuck, 2012), populated with teachers who do not seem to care or value them, an assessment system that pushes them ever lower in terms of esteem, and offers them little more than an avenue to failure. The frustration and lack of trust these students feel are often compounded by the isolation they feel as a result of the failure to form meaningful relationships with the adults in schools. This lack of communication only serves to exacerbate feelings of isolation rather than community and competition for survival over cooperation for the greater good of all (Medoff, 2013; Strike, 2007).

Where there is no trust, there is nothing. Where there is trust, education may begin. Even in the current era of accountability and schooling as commodification, educators can take positive steps to help build the trusting relationships that can disrupt the harms that schooling does to our students. Perhaps, the first action that educators can take to create trusting relationships is to listen to their students. While listening may constitute the initial act, it is not a simple one. Schools are not organized and teachers are not trained to listen to students, yet listening to students humanizes them and gives them dimensions and depth. Students are more than discrete data points or problems in search of correction. They are people with hopes, talents, dreams, laughter, tears, fears, and ideas. To listen to students is to begin to honor them as valued members of a class, a school, and the human race. When students feel listened to in a sincere, nonjudgmental way, they feel more inclined to take the risks needed to form the trusting relationships so critical to real education (Sadowski, 2013)—one that informs a new understanding of smartness. When educators listen, then empathy becomes easier—even to a point where the educator sides with the students rather than against them (Ayers, 2004; Medoff, 2013). With trust, educators can create safe environments where students feel free to do all things—including fail—knowing that they will not be denigrated or reduced. With trust comes cooperation, community, democracy, and education.

Conclusion

Schools in the United States rely on internal mechanisms to perpetuate a seemingly commonsensical understanding of smartness as merit in the quest to quantify learning into an individualistic commodity to be leveraged in, and beyond, the educational marketplace. In this way, students who clear the hurdles have achieved their merit whereas those who fail are expected to blame themselves. This view of smartness as a verb justifies our socioeconomically stratified economy through the narrow lens of merit and bolsters educational policies that operate from this assumption while allowing policy makers to ignore real problems that schooling could help to address of income inequality and systemic racism. This, in turn, has prompted a school culture of test prep, marketization of schools through choice schemes, cultural assimilation, and distrust among policy makers, teachers, and their students. Schools have sorted students into artificial conceptualizations of smartness as they prepare them to assume their place in society.

You can choose to oppose pedagogical practices that seek to reduce teaching into "best practices" for eliciting better indicators of smartness. We suggest that developing a real and meaningful trust with students is the first step in undermining myopic ideologies of smartness that reinforce and reproduce socioeconomic stratification. A society that relies on social demarcations—including socially constructed indicators of smartness—is not a society that relies on trust. If trust existed, we would need no means or methods of sorting individuals into a societal hierarchy. And this is the point for action. If the role of schools, and the educators therein, is to prepare and shape the future society, we as educators must throw off—through trust—myopic and mechanical pedagogical practices that reinforce the illusion of meritocracy. Educators must embrace trust as the first and likely only best practice, as it were, toward fostering an environment where students can experience the liberating educative experience that they deserve. And while there are, to be sure, great educators who trust their students enough to provide those experiences for them, our profession as a whole must begin to insist that students not be characterized by narrow definitions of smartness by way of grades or standardized test scores or that they simply be rule followers. We must make louder the dialogue of holistic education while trusting ourselves and our students enough to invite them into the process.

References

Anyon, J. (1980). Social class and the hidden curriculum of work. *Journal of Education, 162*(1), 67–92.

Anyon, J. (1997). *Ghetto schooling: A political economy of urban educational reform.* Teachers College Press.

Auger, K. A., Shah, S. S., Richardson, T., Hartley, D., Hall, M., Warniment, M., Timmons, K., Bosse, D., Ferris, S. A., Brady, P. W., Schondelmeyer, A. C., & Thompson, J. E. (2020). Association between statewide school closure and COVID-19 incidence and morbidity in the us. *JAMA, 324*(9), 859–870.

Ayers, W. C. (2004). *Teaching toward freedom: Moral and ethical commitment and ethical action in the classroom.* Beacon Publishers.

Baker, K. (2011, Spring). High test scores: The wrong road to national economic success. *Kappa Delta Pi Record, 47*, 116–120.

Baldwin, J. (1963). A talk to teachers. *The Saturday Review.*

BattelleforKids (2019). *Framework for 21st century learning.* http://static.battelleforkids.org/documents/p21/P21_Framework_Brief.pdf

Berlak, A. (2011). Can standardized teacher performance assessment identify highly qualified teachers? In R. Ahlquist, P. C. Gorski, & T. Montano (Eds.), *Assault on kids: How hyper-accountability, corporatization, deficit ideologies, and Ruby Payne are destroying our schools* (pp. 51–62). Peter Lang Publishing.

Bills, D. D. (2004). *The sociology of education and work.* Blackwell Publishing.

Bowles, S., & Gintis, H. (1976). *Schooling in capitalist America.* Harper Collins.

Brewer, T. J., & Myers, P. S. (2015). How neoliberalism subverts equality and perpetuates poverty in our nation's schools. In S. N. Haymes, M. V. d. Haymes, & R. Miller (Eds.), *The Routledge handbook of poverty in the United States* (pp. 190–198). Routledge.

Brewer, T. J., Myers, P. S., & Zhang, M. (2015). Islands unto themselves: How merit pay schemes undermine teacher collaboration. *Critical Questions in Education, 6*(2), 45–54.

Brewer, T. J., & Potterton, A. U. (2020). How market forces and erosion of education as a public good drive equity gaps wider. In M. Soskil (Ed.), *Flip the system us: How teachers can transform education and strengthen American democracy* (pp. 82–96). Routledge.

Brumback, K. (2013). Former Atlanta schools chief indicted in cheating scandal. *Huffington Post*. http://www.huffingtonpost.com/2013/03/29/former-atlanta-schools-chief-indicted_n_2982272.html

Chamberlin, R., Wragg, T., Haynes, G., & Wragg, C. (2002). Performance-related pay and the teaching profession: A review of the literature. *Research Papers in Education, 17*(1), 31–49. doi:10.1080/02671520110102534

Combs, J. P., Edmonson, S., & Harris, S. (2013). *The trust factor: Strategies for school leaders*. Eye on Education.

Courtemanche, C., Garuccio, J., Le, A., Pinkston, J., & Yelowitz, A. (2020). Strong social distancing measures in the United States reduced the COVID-19 growth rate. *Health Measures, 39*(7), 1237–1246.

Delpit, L. (2009). Other people's children: Cultural conflict in the classroom. In C. Kridel (Ed.), *Classic edition sources, education* (4th ed., pp. 69–73). McGraw Hill.

Delpit, L. (2012). *Multiplication is for White people: Raising expectations for other people's children*. The New Press.

EdBuild. (2019). *$23 billion*. EdBuild. https://edbuild.org/content/23-billion/full-report.pdf

Finnigan, T. (2008, January 30). *Merit pay for teachers shows results*. The Daily Signal. http://blog.heritage.org/2008/01/30/merit-pay-for-teachers-shows-results/

Freire, P. (2004). *Pedagogy of indignation*. Paradigm Publishers.

Glass, G. V. (2008). *Fertilizers, pills, and magnet strips: The fate of public education in America*. Information Age Publishing.

Greene, J. P., Forster, G., & Winters, M. A. (2005). *Education myths: What special interest groups want you to believe about our schools—and why it isn't so*. Rowman & Littlefield Publishers.

Grusky, D. B. (Ed.). (2008). *Social stratification: Class, race, and gender in sociological perspective*. Westview Press.

Hatfield, J., & Malkus, N. (2017). *Differences by design? Student composition in charter schools with different academic models*. American Enterprise Institute. Retrieved from https://www.aei.org/research-products/report/differences-by-design-student-composition-in-charter-schools-with-different-academic-models/

Hatt, B. (2012). Smartness as a cultural practice in schools. *American Educational Research Journal, 49*(3), 438–460.

Head, J. R., Andrejko, K., Cheng, Q., Collender, P. A., Phillips, S., Boser, A., Heaney, A. K., Hoover, C. M., Wu, S. L., Northrup, G. R., Click, K., Harrison, R., Lewnard, J. A., & Remais, J. V. (2020). The effect of school closures and reopening strategies on COVID-19 infection dynamics in the San Francisco Bay area: A cross-sectional survey and modeling analysis. *medRxiv*. doi:10.1101/2020.08.06.20169797

Herrnstein, R. J., & Murray, C. (1994). *The bell curve: Intelligence and class structure in American life*. The Free Press.

Horn, J. (2011). Corporatism, KIPP, and cultural eugenics. In P. E. Kovacs (Ed.), *The Gates foundation and the future of U.S. "Public" schools* (pp. 80–103). Routledge.

Jencks, C., & Phillips, M. (Eds.). (1998). *The Black–White test score gap*. Brookings Institution Press.

Jencks, C., Smith, M., Acland, H., Bane, M. J., Cohen, D., Gintis, H., Heyns, B., & Michelson, S. (1972). *Inequality: A reassessment of the effect of family and schooling in America*. Basic Books.

Knoester, M. (Ed.). (2012). *International struggles for critical democratic education*. Peter Lang.

Korp, H. (2011). What counts as being smart around here? The performance of smartness and masculinity in vocational upper secondary education. *Education, Citizenship and Social Justice, 6*(21), 21–37.

Kozol, J. (1991). *Savage inequalities: Children in America's schools*. Crown Publishing Group.

Labaree, D. (1988). *The making of an American high school: The credentials market & the Central High School of Philadelphia, 1838–1939*. Yale University Press.

Labaree, D. (1997a). *How to succeed in school without really learning: The credentials race in American education*. Yale University Press.

Labaree, D. (1997b). Public goods, private goods: The American struggle over educational goals. *American Educational Research Journal, 34*(1), 39–81.

Ladner, M., & Myslinski, D. (2013). *Report card on American education: Ranking state k–12 performance, progress, and reform* American Legislative Exchange Council. Retrieved from https://www.alec.org/app/uploads/2015/12/18th_Report_Card.pdf

Maier, A. (2012). Doing good and doing well: Credentialism and teach for America. *Journal of Teacher Education, 63*(1), 10–22. doi:10.1177/0022487111422071

Markovits, D. (2019). *The meritocracy trap: How America's foundational myth feeds inequality, dismantles the middle class, and devours the elite*. Penguin Press.

Markow, D., Macia, L., & Lee, H. (2013). *The MetLife survey of the American teacher: Challenges for school leadership*. MetLife. https://www.metlife.com/content/dam/microsites/about/corporate-profile/MetLife-Teacher-Survey-2012.pdf

Markow, D., & Pieters, A. (2012). *The MetLife survey of the American teacher: Teachers, parents, and the economy*. MetLife. https://www.metlife.com/assets/cao/contributions/foundation/american-teacher/MetLife-Teacher-Survey-2011.pdf

Massey, D. S. (2007). *Categorically unequal: The American stratification system*. Russell Sage Foundation.

Massey, D. S., & Denton, N. A. (1993). *American apartheid: Segregation and the making of the underclass*. Harvard University Press.

McLaren, P. (2011). If there is anyone out there . . . In P. R. Carr & B. J. Porfilio (Eds.), *The phenomenon of Obama and the agenda for education: Can hope audaciously trump neoliberalism?* (pp. 265–285). Information Age.

Medoff, L. (2013). Getting beyond "I hate math." *Educational Leadership, 71*(1), 44–48.

Muller, J. Z. (2018). *The tyranny of metrics*. Princeton University Press.

National Commission on Excellence in Education. (1983). *A nation at risk: The imperative for educational reform*. Washington, DC: National Commission on Excellence in Education.

Protsik, J. (1995). History of teacher pay and incentive reforms. *Journal of School Leadership, 6*(3), 265–289.

Ravitch, D. (2010). *The death and life of the great American school system: How testing and choice are undermining education*. Basic Books.

Ravitch, D. (2013). *Reign of error: The hoax of the privatization movement and the danger to America's public schools*. Knopf.

Sacks, P. (1999). *Standardized minds: The high price of America's testing culture and what we can do to change it*. Da Capo Press.

Sadowski, M. (2013). *Portraits of promise: Voices of successful immigrant students*. Harvard Education Press.

Sennett, R., & Cobb, J. (1973). *The hidden injuries of class*. Vintage Books.

Silverman, M., Sibbald, R., & Stranges, S. (2020). Ethics of COVID-19-related school closures. *Canadian Journal of Public Health, 111*(4), 462–465.

Springer, M. G., Ballou, D., Hamilton, L., Le, V.-N., Lockwood, J. R., McCaffrey, D. F., Pepper, M., & Stecher, B. M. (2010). *Teacher pay performance: Experimental evidence from the project on incentives in teaching*. National Center on Performance Incentives. http://www.rand.org/content/dam/rand/pubs/reprints/2010/RAND_RP1416.pdf

Strike, K. A. (2007). *Ethical leadership in schools: Creating community in an environment of accountability*. Corwin.

Tuck, E. (2012). *Urban youth and school pushout: Gateways, get-aways, and the GED*. Routledge.

Tyack, D., & Cuban, L. (1995). Tinkering toward utopia: A century of public school reform. In C. Kridel (Ed.), *Classic edition sources, education* (pp. 175–179). McGraw Hill.

Walberg, H. J., & Bast, J. L. (2003). *Education and capitalism: How overcoming our fear of markets and economics can improve America's schools*. Hoover Institution Press.

Wink, J. (2005). *Critical pedagogy: Notes from the real world*. Pearson.

Chapter Five

CREATING AND COMMODIFYING THE NEOLIBERAL SELF:

A WEBERIAN ANALYSIS OF AN INTERNATIONAL EDUCATION COURSE

by Ashlee B. Anderson & Andrea Arce-Trigatti

U.S. children are stuck in a rigid system of schooling based on hallmark neoliberal trends like standards, accountability, and competition (Apple, 2005; Spring, 2015, 2017). This system of schooling has a profound impact on how students perceive themselves and the world around them. Using one undergraduate course in international education as an example, this chapter examines how the seemingly rational organization of existing school structures preclude correct understandings and practices of learning, as well as the places where value is located, via Max Weber's (2002) conceptions of the Protestant ethic and "shell as hard as steel" (p. 121). The conceptual model that our teacher candidates have of school is linked to the way that they believe learning happens (Anderson, 2013; Shapiro, 2013). This chapter, then, rests on understanding teacher candidates' apprehension regarding truly educative practices in teaching, constructivist ones that leverage collaboration and social interaction.

The existing conceptual model arose from a neoliberal regime that envisions the privatization of public institutions, including schools, to achieve the perceived advantages of the private sector (e.g., efficiency, excellence, and accountability; Spring, 2017).

Scholars have identified such reforms as creating an audit culture supported by a sort of "new managerialism." In this scheme, social institutions become corporatized via policies and practices based on the assumption that the vital considerations of learning processes are cost, competition, and, arising from these, surveillance and measurement (Apple, 2005; Clarke, 2004). Each of the agents and attributes in this system becomes a measurable commodity, as opposed to part of a relationship of meaningful subjects.

To address what happens to people ensconced in commodified circumstances, we use Weber's (2002) conceptions of the Protestant ethic and "shell as hard as steel." In so doing, we describe how individuals reconstitute their own assumptions and values, and thus live their lives, as a function of their positioning in this world as commodities that are expressed as personal material wealth. That is, their own assumptions and values come to validate the very capitalist mission that constrains them within commodification.

Next, as a way of providing an example of this in practice, we highlight one undergraduate course in international education that we both teach as an example of how these theoretical processes play out (Anderson, 2013; Shapiro, 2013). As course objectives include exposing teacher candidates to diverse forms of thinking and complex issues, we leverage constructivist-inspired strategies to facilitate collaboration and dialogue (Anderson, 2013; Shapiro, 2013). However, because of how thoroughly they have been socialized into the neoliberal paradigm of schooling, the teacher candidates overwhelmingly prefer techniques featuring control, limited peer engagement, and compliance with a prescribed set of criteria on which they will be independently assessed. That is, our teacher candidates attempt to apply the same interpretive frameworks to which they have been exposed in their own educational histories to the alternative strategies that we attempt to share. Because their experience is couched in the logic of rationality and assessment, any departure becomes, therefore, unthinkable.

We conclude that neoliberal reform has been successful in fundamentally altering how teacher candidates view themselves and their positions in modern society (Baeher, 2001). We find that the ultimate outcome of this process is the objectification and subsequent commodification of students in pursuit of the neoliberal mission. To be more specific, we argue that students actively commodify themselves via their internalization of existing education structures that function according to the Protestant ethic and encase them in a "shell as hard as steel" (Baeher, 2001). One vital challenge that educators face, then, is to understand how people actually learn and then attempt to align the audit culture with core concepts that need to be taken away from engaging with complex subjects. We conclude the chapter with implications for pedagogy that incorporate examples of strategies we have developed to engage teacher candidates more collectively and dialogically. We suggest that, by applying such strategies, we can transcend our own surrender to commodification.

Neoliberal Reform, The Audit Culture, And The "New Managerialism"

Since the 1980s, neoliberal reformers have been fundamentally altering the ways in which the public sector operates, favoring, instead, the perceived advantages of the private sector (e.g., excellence, efficiency, and accountability; Spring, 2015, 2017). In schools this has been operationalized by, for example, the increasing roles of standards, high-stakes systems of accountability, and school choice policies These features are consistent with what Apple (2005) describes as an audit culture that has changed how individuals view themselves. As an example, Apple (2005) states,

> Neo-liberalism requires the constant production of evidence that you are doing things "efficiently" and in the "correct" way. . . . This situation has given rise to what might best be called an *audit culture*. . . . The widespread nature of these evaluative and measurement pressures, and their ability to become parts of our common sense, crowd out other conceptions of

> effectiveness and democracy. . . . The ultimate result of an auditing culture of this kind is not the promised de-centralisation that plays such a significant role rhetorically in most neoliberal self-understandings, but what seems to be a massive re-centralisation and what is best seen as a process of de-democratisation. (pp. 14–15, emphasis in original)

Neoliberalism demands the marketization and corporatization of the state's public functions that demand a high level of surveillance on the ground (audit culture). In the case of schooling, this manifests in reforms based on high-stakes testing, continuous evaluation, standards, and the like, which challenge key features of democracy including diverse forms of expression, meaning arising through qualitative dialogue, critical thinking, and collaboration. What is more, this audit culture has taken on a sense of common sense, wherein other understandings become unintelligible. As Apple (2005) reminds us, "for it to be successful, our common sense must be changed so that we see the world only as individual consumers and we see ourselves as surrounded by a world in which everything is potentially a commodity for sale" (pp. 16–17).

To address how and by whom these processes are operationalized, Apple (2005) speaks of a "new managerialism":

> A good deal of the current emphasis on audits and more rigorous forms of accountability, on tighter control, and a vision that competition will lead to greater efficiency . . . comes from educational managers and bureaucratic officers who fully believe that such control is warranted and "good." Not only do these forms of control have an extremely long history in education, but tighter control, high-stakes testing, and (reductive) accountability methods provide more dynamic roles for such managers. (p. 20)

One look at the expanded bureaucracy of modern schooling and the mechanisms of quality control that have been established are evidence enough of this. The bureaucratization of schooling then, scaffolded by the creation of this "new managerial" class, has fundamentally altered how we view schooling, which, in turn, has altered how we view ourselves (Apple, 2005). The rationalization process has transformed the artifacts of this system, including students and the teachers, into commodities, a process consistent with Weber's (2002) conceptions of the Protestant ethic and "shell as hard as steel."

Theoretical Framework

Max Weber and *The Protestant Ethic*

Max Weber, a German sociologist and political economist from the turn of the 20th century, is commonly regarded as one of the founding architects of modern sociology, a credit that is, in part, a consequence of the widespread distribution of Weber's (2002) now canonical text *The Protestant Ethic and the Spirit of Capitalism* (hereafter, *The Protestant Ethic*). With *The Protestant Ethic*, Weber introduces various cultural aspects that, he believes, had a hand in the eventual rise of capitalism in the West, specifically those resulting from the religious expansion of Protestantism in 16th- and 17th-century Europe. For Weber, the advent of Protestant religions after the Reformation, especially Calvinism, fostered the conditions that would ultimately validate the capitalist enterprise. Basing his claims on the historical particularities of the Reformation in concert with the expansion of economic activities in northern Europe, Weber concluded that capitalism was, in fact, the ultimate consequence of Christianity's reboot after the 16th-century schism.

The Calvinist concept of predestination provides a particularly useful example of the intricacies of this process. According to this principle, because God is omniscient, an individual's savior/damnation is predetermined at birth. Also, the likelihood that individuals are destined for admittance into heaven would most certainly be reflected in their mortal lives. As a result, a person who is in God's favor would exhibit some visible expressions of success in the mortal plane. Because the outward appearance of wealth is a powerful indicator of a successful life and because God would not reward an evil person with success, the visible performance of wealth would likely indicate salvation. Because this is so, individuals who are favored by God would also be inclined to actively pursue wealth through hard work and self-discipline. This stands in marked contrast to the outward rejection of worldly wealth that was standard to Christianity prior to the Reformation and, ironically, the message shared by Jesus. In the ultimate example of a self-fulfilling prophecy, the outcome of predestination is the establishment of a dynamic process wherein individuals, wanting to reflect that they are favored by God, reconstitute their lives to focus on wealth acquisition. Societally, this pursuit gets rendered as positive, even sacred, and so the capitalist order is validated (Weber, 2002).[1]

The ways in which the relationship between man and nature was fundamentally altered by the introduction of the Protestant ethic facilitated the reorientation of social life towards the perceived advantages of capitalism, a shift which culminated in the creation of new frameworks to structure social life. Although not currently religious in its substance and divorced from what Calvin likely had in mind when he developed the concept of predestination, the Protestant ethic has been assimilated into social and cultural consciousness to such an extent that its preferred practices have justified a capitalist orientation. It has become a structural condition, wherein individuals exist through economic activity, not apart from it. In many ways, then, the reality that we experience in the West is not so much the result of our own independent creation, as it is a consequence of the kind of control paradigm that functions according to the Protestant ethic. It is a consequence of what Parsons translates as the "iron cage" (Weber, 1930, p. 181).

The "iron cage," a highly recognizable sociological concept attributed to Weber, is the ultimate consequence of modern capitalism. Introduced by Talcott Parsons in his 1930 translation of the original German *stahlhartes Gehäuse*, the phrase describes the ways in which the Protestant ethic has been subsumed into the public psyche to such an extent that individuals become bound to it, without ever recognizing the control paradigm of which it is but one consequence. When religious devotion became connected with outward displays of wealth according to the Protestant ethic, the newly formed economic system assumed a public and moral legitimation, despite the ways in which it was able to institute new, albeit hidden, mechanisms of control based on the perceived advantages of rationalization, bureaucracy, and technicality. The ultimate outcome, then, is the creation of an "iron cage" that constrains us and makes concepts outside of the discourse of the capitalist order unseeable, unthinkable, and thus unknowable.[2]

Weber and Neoliberalism

The connections between the "shell as hard as steel" and the commonsense logic of neoliberal policies/practices favoring an audit culture based on bureaucratic rationality cannot be overstated—particularly in the world of teacher preparation and in the practice of teaching within an overly bureaucratic system. In fact, Weber explicitly connected education with bureaucracy via an examination culture that has developed as the logical mechanism by which to sort individuals into their "natural" positions within modern bureaucracies. For example, Weber positions examinations as the means by which to ensure fiscally advantageous credentials and, in so doing, advances the infrastructure of modern capitalism via a standardized and rationally organized bureaucracy. By extension, the sort of audit culture theorized by Apple (2005) represents one normative outgrowth of this system. Taken as a whole, then, the "shell as hard as steel" creates "*a new kind of being*" who, despite possessing agency, understands and embraces education as a tool of capitalist (and so neoliberal) oppression (Baeher, 2001, p. 153). In the process, these new beings effectively commodify themselves via, for example, participating in and ultimately upholding the kind of examination culture that not only becomes normalized, in part, as the result of the status and wealth that it proffers but also exploits and fetters them. This examination culture (and the "shell as hard as steel"), then, is entirely consistent with Apple's (2005) description of an audit culture designed to further a neoliberal mission.

The "Shell As Hard As Steel" In Practice: Lessons From An International Education Course

In the context of education, the "shell as hard as steel" provides a useful tool for analyzing the public legitimation of education reform efforts based on the perceived advantages of external accountability systems (as opposed to intrinsic motivation), business models of inputs and outputs, and the assumed rationality of standardized tests and rubrics. As an example, we provide a brief case example of an undergraduate course we teach in international education in an attempt to highlight the ways in which the seemingly rational organization of existing reform trends preclude alternative understandings/practices of teacher candidate learning, as well as the places where value is located. The purpose of this section is twofold: First, we overview various pedagogical strategies that we use to scaffold teacher candidate learning: constructivism and collaboration. Next, we provide a background of teacher candidates' reactions to course content and requirements as they are overlaid on our pedagogical decisions, paying special attention to connect to our initial point of the "shell as hard as steel" in the context of education. This provides insight into neoliberal policy reforms that legitimize certain forms of learning in the eyes of those who are being educated.

The Pedagogical Theories: Constructivism and Collaboration

In an effort to capitalize on the diversity that this course attracts—both in teacher candidate disciplines and in the topics that are discussed—we leverage constructivist inspired strategies to facilitate collaboration and dialogue (Anderson, 2013; Shapiro, 2013). Constructivism is rooted in the idea that knowledge construction can occur through continual social interaction and exposure to various perspectives (Anderson, 2013)—in effect, this approach stands in contrast to "hard as steel" and audit culture characterizing K–12 education. Rather than focus on training teachers to adhere to myopic understandings of curriculum, teaching, and learning, the course features the following teamwork objective: Teacher candidates will work in a team-like environment and strive to appreciate and incorporate the perspectives of their peers in their learning. As the topics we develop are quite complex and ever-changing, it is our belief that utilizing a social constructivist approach to teaching these topics will help teacher candidates appreciate the multidimensional elements that these topics bring, particularly when they are conceptualized as international education policy (Anderson, 2013; Shapiro, 2013). Scholarship also supports the use of constructivist approaches to learning complex material, underscoring that such interaction has shown to increase teacher candidate engagement, motivate self-regulatory behavior, and increase interest in the content (Alderman, 2004; Anderson, 2013; Shapiro, 2013).

This learning theory is therefore a cornerstone of collaboration in learning. Adopting the approach that teacher candidates can and should learn from one another, a collaborative learning experience can provide teacher candidates with the opportunity to engage in meaningful discussions that lead to the exposure of new ideas, new insights, and, ultimately, growth (Anderson, 2013). However, such learning environments are dependent on teacher candidates' own conceptualizations of learning and their motivation to share, engage, and build knowledge off others' ideas (Alderman, 2004). Furthermore, Shapiro (2013) underscores that collaborative learning is dependent on the type of experiences teacher candidates encounter, suggesting that intentional interaction and meaning-making experiences aligned with the lesson's overall objectives are a vital part of this type of environment and overall growth.

Understanding Teacher Candidates' Conceptualizations of Collaboration

In accordance, before engaging in collaborative learning, it is necessary to gauge teacher candidates' understanding, and potential appreciation, for collaboration. In the course featured here, to assess the teacher candidates' understanding of what they are supposed to take away from collaborative learning (i.e., fostering engaging conversations and developing critical thinking skills), one of the authors has the teacher candidates fill out a survey regarding the purposes of group work. As long as the survey has been completed, teacher candidates overwhelmingly indicate that their preferred method for engaging in group projects is not to learn from one another but rather to understand their part of the project, understand what they are being graded on, and ensure that everyone is doing their portion with respect to these guidelines. In doing so, teacher candidates attempt to apply the same interpretive frameworks to which they have been exposed in their own educational histories to new forms of learning.

For example, when initially asked to identify the purpose of group work in the form of an open-ended question, the top 10 most commonly listed answers (in order) include the following key terms/phrases: promote collaboration, promote the ability to work with diverse sets of people, promote creativity, work towards a common goal, the inclusion of more than just one idea, enhance communication skills, create relationships, learn from others, teamwork, and work skills (skills to find a job). However, in following multiple-choice questions, the answers teacher candidates provide offer a different perspective of how they would ideally engage in this type of collaborative learning environment. For example, regarding the question, "While working on a group project I like to . . . ," overwhelmingly teacher candidates selected the response "Make sure that if I am doing my part, others are completing their own part as well," over other, more collaborative, responses including "Work together towards the final product" or "Incorporate what I have learned from others to the larger project." On another question that asked teacher candidates how they typically engage in group project work, again, teacher candidate selections indicated a preference for answers reflecting individual effort that was then pieced together with others' individual efforts (e.g., "Understand what I am being graded on and base my contribution on the rubric"; "Understand the essential parts of the project and piece my part together with others").

Finally, perhaps the most resounding teacher candidate selections came from the question gauging how teacher candidates understand the success of a group project. Once more, teacher candidates tended to choose the most individualistic option (i.e., "If we did everything required of us from the rubric then we accomplished our task") over more collaborative options (i.e., "Create something new from differing ideas"; "Learn something from one another"). A dichotomy, therefore, exists between an initial understanding of the purpose and value of group work versus how teacher candidates indicate how they engage with group work. We argue that this is reflective of the reification of individualistic accountability measures that have been engrained in our teacher candidates' perceptions of learning, even within a constructivist, collaborative environment. We also contend that intentional interaction and meaning-making experiences, as suggested by Shapiro (2013), are necessary to address this dichotomy within this class.

Pedagogical Strategies and Activities

Understanding teacher candidates' initial reactions to collaboration thus helps plan the lessons they will engage with throughout the course. These reactions also offer a way to reach benchmarks and objectives that help achieve the type of constructivist collaboration we aim to accomplish via the lessons taught. The course design thus reflects this collaborative, pedagogical intention via the organization of the content and the assignments developed as requirements. This is accomplished via two different learning experiences: (1) progression through theoretical training that helps them identify individualistic, neoliberal tendencies and (2) extensive group projects throughout the progression of the course.

Theoretical Training

Related to the first learning experience, a scaffolded design that features three major perspectives is introduced to teacher candidates as a major cornerstone of the course. In the first level, critical theory is taught as it relates to neoliberalism and progressive humanism (Spring, 2017). Teacher candidates become familiar with education policy as it manifests in American educational contexts, and they are asked to engage in various assignments that make connections between theory and their own contexts (Anderson, 2013). This level features intensive teacher candidate discussion, in-class group-work activities, and individual self-reflection. As part of this learning experience, teacher candidates are asked to engage with various policy outcomes and compare those to their own experiences, examining the advantages and disadvantages of more individualistic, neoliberal approaches in contrast to more holistic, progressive approaches (Spring, 2015). Through these activities, they gain insight into how their own experiences might have changed should the structure of their school system have encompassed non-punitive, supportive policies in lieu of competitive accountability outcomes (i.e., lessened test anxiety, less stress, more interest in diverse topics, teachers who were less stressed).

As the course progresses, this learning experience is expanded to include the conceptualizations of neoliberalism and progressive policies as they manifest in other countries. In this part of the course, we teach about developed and developing nation contexts via 10 international case studies meant to scaffold the teacher candidates' creation of two major group projects. For these, teacher candidates are asked to develop a hypothetical school system that addresses three major educational policy issues within both developed and developing contexts, that is, absenteeism, teacher training, opportunity gaps, inequitable funding structures, access to quality education, and so forth, via discussions of five major components: goals and curricula, structure, staffing, accountability, and community. The final product for each of these two projects is a written report highlighting these five items and how they address the original three policy issues assigned. Once more, through applying theoretical aspects into their work, teacher candidates are asked to examine and critique the advantages and disadvantages of an individualistic, neoliberal system in comparison to a holistic, progressive system. From this, teacher candidates find that progressive systems tend to feature more balanced student and teacher experiences, more holistic measures that assist all schools (both struggling and succeeding) while offering students and their families a renewed engagement with school that is more community-oriented (Spring, 2015).

Extensive Group Projects

The second part of the learning experience focuses on the collaborative aspects of the group projects. As part of these group projects, teacher candidates engage in several team-building exercises geared toward establishing a collaborative environment in what Johnson and Johnson (1999) define as effective cooperative learning. This type of cooperative learning encourages positive interdependence, individual accountability, face-to-face promotive interaction, social skills, and group processing (Johnson & Johnson, 1999). Requisites for the completion of these projects include several complementary assignments that speak to these elements, including (a) a group grade linked to the seamless, edited written and oral product (positive interdependence); (b) a portion of the grade that assesses individual contributions via peer evaluation (individual accountability); (c) designated group workdays (face-to-face promotive interaction); (d) group contracts or agreement of cooperation forms (social skills); and (e) group check-ins (group processing; Johnson & Johnson, 1999).

Teacher Candidate Progress and Engagement

Although teacher candidates initially struggle with the conceptualization of collaborative learning as engineered from these assignments and experiences, the way that they engage with the projects typically shifts from the first to the second project. For example, teacher candidates initially tend to adopt an individualistic approach to their first course project. This may be reflected in dividing the work of the project so that they do not need to engage with one another, assessing one another solely based on their individual responsibilities, taking days off to work individually on the group-work days, and only signing one group contract. By the time we check in with teacher candidate groups on the first project, we see a strain in time management (i.e., not meeting deadlines and nothing in the contract to penalize this type of activity), inconsistencies with quality of work (i.e., what teacher candidates mean by a page of contribution varies), and miscommunication between the group members on how the contract responsibilities are outlined (i.e., who ends up editing and how is the workload divided).

To avoid these issues in the second group project, groups tend to make major adjustments to their work habits, dividing the work more evenly and through an iterative approach, coming to class and meeting as a group on group workdays, and constantly adjusting the contract to reflect varying levels of increased positive interdependence. By the time we check in with these groups, the work is more reflective of collaborative exchanges, with projects flowing better and teacher candidate voices being more integrated than the first group project. Through these types of activities, then, teacher candidates are exposed to a different type of learning environment than what is traditionally fostered in the K–12 setting, wherein individual assignments and inter-classroom competition are the norm (Johnson & Johnson, 1999; Shapiro, 2013). Therefore, not only are they gaining knowledge about the type of theoretical policy aspects introduced at the beginning of the course, but they are also actively engaging in the type of collaborative atmosphere that is reflective of constructivist learning environments.

Creating And Commodifying The Neoliberal Self

Nearly all the teacher candidates whom we teach have experienced schooling under No Child Left Behind, a 2001 legislative act that dictated the expanded use of consequential assessment practices, standards, rubrics, and data to inform market processes. This type of framework runs counter to our own constructivist pedagogies, anchored primarily on fostering critical thinking and dialogue, a disconnect that ultimately results in dissonance between teacher candidates' experience and their interaction with a structure that exists outside of their learning norms. As noted, we posit that because this world is rooted in the belief and value of the logic of rationality and assessment, any departure becomes, therefore, unthinkable. Thus, one of the vital challenges that we face as instructors for this course is to understand how our teacher candidates learn and attempt to align this "checkbox" mentality with the core concepts that need to be taken away from engaging with subjects as messy as the ones we discuss. Ultimately, these processes are reflective of the ways in which the "shell as hard as steel" and policies that espouse the perceived advantages of a rationally organized and efficient system of education serve to alter how we view ourselves and our positions in modern society.

There is no question that schools serve as powerful institutions that socialize individuals and teach them acceptable societal norms. Because existing neoliberal reforms, which are supported by what Apple (2005) labels a "new managerial" class, are the primary mechanism by which schooling is currently delivered, students are positioned as objects that can be manipulated to support existing economic structures. They become commodities by which reformers advance an economic agenda. What is more, in their support of neoliberal reforms (as evidenced by, for example, their activities in our course), students effectively consent to their own commodification. That is, they internalize existing education structures that function according to the Protestant ethic encasing them in a "shell as hard as steel"; in so doing, they advance a neoliberal mission that becomes self-perpetuating (Apple, 2005; Baeher, 2001). It becomes the task of educators, then, to break this cycle via pedagogical practices that challenge the socialization processes by which students become commodified.

Thinking Outside Of Themselves: Pedagogical Strategies

Pedagogy is ultimately a reflective process that necessitates that instructors understand the connection between the learning strategies they are utilizing and the idiosyncrasies associated with their implementation. In understanding how to improve a pedagogy geared toward a constructivist learning framework, it is also pertinent that instructors are aware of what the challenges may be for students that exist in a "shell as hard as steel" regarding their learning habits. Although it is unrealistic to believe that instructors can reshape the more than 12 years of neoliberal-inspired instruction our teacher candidates receive, which reflects the simplification of learning to mere inputs and outputs, there are certain pedagogical strategies that can be leveraged to help teacher candidates break from this shell. The implications of this work for postsecondary pedagogical strategies are thus founded on ideas that could potentially address this type of dichotomy between theoretically understanding the role of constructivism and collaboration in learning versus how teacher candidates actually believe they need to learn.

The first implication is geared toward recalibrating complementary assignments aimed toward developing Johnson and Johnson's (1999) five basic elements for cooperative work. Although we have designed the course with the purpose of ensuring that these elements are a salient part of the group-work requisite for this class, this is often teacher candidates' first interaction with such types of cooperative learning elements. As a result, teacher candidates have indicated that they view these elements more like busywork rather than a vital part of successful cooperative learning projects, lessening the amount of effort or work placed into these activities. It then falls on the instructors to help make the connection between taking these elements seriously and ultimate success with the final product (Sawyer, 2006). This could be accomplished in a training session provided for teacher candidates as part of one of the group workdays or as a separate lab section offered for those interested in improving their teamwork skills. This sort of training would, of course, need to be scaffolded by continuous opportunities for group engagement. That is, group work would need to be a fundamental element of the course as a whole that is supported by continuous and varied group activities.

Teacher candidates' understanding of cooperative work could also be evaluated on the level of complexity associated with their group's contributions to these complementary group assignments. To clarify, teacher candidates' work on these assignments would be evaluated on the level of cooperation or collaboration that they reflect, requiring teacher candidates to learn and distinguish the differences between group work as a pseudo-individual assignment and as a project that leverages positive interdependence (Johnson & Johnson, 1999). In this regard, group contracts could be graded based on how the responsibilities are divided and if those divisions are reflective of interconnected responsibilities or if they were purposefully designed to decrease the amount of time teacher candidates spend working together on the project. This type of feedback would provide an iterative process for learning how these assignments work toward creating effective group processes (Sawyer, 2006). To accomplish this, teacher candidates must, again, be taught these differences within a training session or supplementary lab, how this varies from what they are accustomed to, and why it is important for their learning within a collaborative environment (Sawyer, 2006).

Finally, another pedagogical implication leverages the last item that teacher candidates identified as the purpose of group work on the survey featured in this contribution: the development of work skills. This response from teacher candidates overwhelmingly reflects the inherent association that they have of learning as linked to an economic benefit rather than as a step toward progressing their personal growth (Spring, 2015, 2017). Thus, if teacher candidates are already inclined to adopt neoliberal strategies for learning as accurate and effective, it would behoove instructors wanting to develop this type of constructivist environment to have teacher candidates unpack this association and critically think about how they understand collaboration regarding learning (Preston & Aslett, 2013; Sawyer, 2006). Preston and Aslett (2013) contend that pedagogical practices that leverage reflection in a way that helps teacher candidates analyze behavior and engagement shifts pertaining to these ideas are a form of activist pedagogy often needed in courses that feature a social justice curriculum in the context of neoliberal learning. Self-reflection and evaluation in this regard may, therefore, help teacher candidates identify and better comprehend this dichotomy, as well as equipping them with actionable ways to engage with group work conducive to collaborative learning (Preston & Aslett, 2013). We attempt to leverage this particular strategy by, at the very outset of and throughout the course, asking teacher candidates not only to reflect on their own educational histories but also to consider the biases that they bring to our classroom space and their perceptions of what education *should* look like. Certainly, this takes a good deal of time to unpack and discuss, but we've found that it gets them closer to thinking outside of themselves.

Notes

1. "Innerworldly Protestant asceticism works with all its force against the uninhibited *enjoyment* of possessions; it discourages *consumption*, especially the consumption of luxuries. Conversely, it has the effect of liberating the *acquisition of wealth* from the inhibitions of traditionalist ethics; it breaks the fetters on the striving for gain by not only legalizing it, but (in the sense described) seeing it as directly willed by God" (Weber, 2002, p. 115, emphasis in original).

2. The notion of how concepts become unthinkable because of the dominance of a paradigm has been elaborated in other scholarly traditions as well. For instance, in the introduction to this book, Harman mentions Foucault's conception of discourse, in which a dominant discourse functions to make alternative discourses unimaginable.

References

Alderman, M. K. (2004). *Motivation for achievement: Possibilities for teaching and learning* (2nd ed). Erlbaum.

Anderson, H. (2013). Collaborative learning communities: A postmodern perspective on teaching and learning. In B. J. Irby, G. Brown, R. Lara-Alecio, & S. Jackson (Eds.), *The handbook of educational theories* (pp. 515–527). Information Age Publishing.

Apple, M. W. (2005). Education, markets, and an audit culture. *Critical Quarterly, 47*(1–2), 11–29.

Baeher, P. (2001). The "iron cage" and the "shell as hard as steel": Parsons, Weber, and the *stahlhartes gehäuse* metaphor in *The Protestant Ethic and the Spirit of Capitalism. History and Theory, 40*(2), 153–169.

Clarke, J. (2004). Dissolving the public realm? The logics and limits of neo-liberalism. *Journal of Social Policy, 33*(1), 27–48.

Johnson, D. W., & Johnson, R. T. (1999). Making cooperative learning work. *Theory Into Practice, 28*(2), 67–73.

Preston, S., & Aslett, J. (2013). Resisting neoliberalism from within the academy: Subversion through an activist pedagogy. *Social Work Education: The International Journal, 33*(4), 502–518.

Sawyer, K. (2006). Preface. In K. Sawyer (Ed.), *The Cambridge handbook of the learning sciences* (pp. xi–xiii). Cambridge University Press.

Shapiro, A. (2013). A theory and practice of constructivist curriculum. In B. J. Irby, G. Brown, R. Lara-Alecio, & S. Jackson (Eds.), *The handbook of educational theories* (pp. 317–328). Information Age Publishing.

Spring, J. H. (2015). *Globalization of education: An introduction.* Taylor & Francis.

Spring, J. H. (2017). *Political agendas for education: From make America great again to stronger together.* Routledge.

Weber, M. (1930). *The Protestant ethic and the spirit of capitalism* (T. Parsons, Trans.). G. Allen & Unwin.

Weber, M. (2002). *The Protestant ethic and the 'spirit' of capitalism and other writings* (P. Baeher & G. C. Wells, Eds. & Trans.). Penguin Books.

Chapter Six

COMBATING THE COMMODIFICATION OF KNOWLEDGE: THE MAKER MOVEMENT

by Michael Schad & Kurt Stemhagen

Introduction: The Market As Worldview

> Commodity: "A comparatively homogeneous product that can typically be bought in bulk. It usually refers to a raw material - oil, cotton, cocoa, silver - but can also describe a manufactured product used to make other things, for example, microchips used in personal computers. Commodities are often traded on commodity exchanges."
>
> —*The Economist*

Faith in the power of markets to make our lives better runs deep. In this chapter, we call attention to the ways in which education has been commodified through reverence for the free market. After considering some of the problems of knowledge commodification, we then turn to the maker movement, presenting it as one way that this commodification can be resisted. The maker movement is a social movement embedded with constructivist principles that imparts knowledge creation through the creation of learner-centered objects. It has the potential to help teachers enact pedagogies that tend toward engaged contextualized knowing and away from abstract and dehumanized commodified versions of knowledge.[1] We make the case that the maker movement has the potential to disrupt neoliberal commodification.

Viewing knowledge as a commodity, in some ways, fits with what we are socialized to consider common sense. Unexamined ways of thinking about education tend to conceptualize knowledge as a set of objects, available for us to acquire and put away in our minds in atomized and standard pieces, as if our minds were drawers or warehouses or bank vaults. Freire's (2000) choice of language in his critique of the traditional model of education, in fact, refers to it as a "banking" model of education, and he highlights problems that accompany the assumption that learning can be equated to filling up empty accounts with units of knowledge. While not the sole cause of the commodification of knowledge, we argue that the rise of the market metaphor has provided a very favorable climate for the popularizing of this largely counterproductive way of thinking about learning and knowledge.

Knowledge As Commodity And Currency

There are troublesome effects of assuming that market metaphors accurately describe how things really are, and even worse, how this ends up as the foundation of a worldview. Knowledge commodification is one particularly problematic effect of market metaphors. Large-scale experiments in free-market K–12 education have been taking place in city school systems in the United States for some time now. Philadelphia was an early site as the state took control of the schools in the early 21st century in response to years of what was widely considered subpar performance. We share this example because it provides a clear illustration of some of the negative possible consequences of adopting restricted views of knowledge and what learning is/should be. Two years into the experiment, the market was being credited with improving the education of Philadelphia's young people. An Associated Press story from that era reported that

> as Philadelphia's 214,000 public school students finished their regular classes last week, there were reasons for hope in the city's beleaguered system: test scores were up for a second straight year and the district had its first balanced budget in seven years. (Caruso, 2004, p. 18)

From the start of this movement, the criteria by which the quality of education was being judged were rising test scores and financial solvency. No word was mentioned about educational successes associated with the curriculum in the same district. However, 2 years prior to the privatization experiment, Philadelphia's superintendent, David Hornbeck (2000) promoted a districtwide service-learning project, touting how students were "intellectually engaged and personally empowered" and reported teachers feeling "inspired, creative, and passionate" (p. 665). Why were successes of the service-learning experiment not mentioned in the news stories about the Philadelphia schools' progress in the wake of their switch to a free-market model? Assuming Hornbeck wrote truthfully about service learning's benefits, we see two possible explanations, both of which are likely in play:

1. Intellectual engagement/personal empowerment as student outcomes are not easily commodifiable and, as a result, go unreported.
2. In pushing to demonstrate that Philadelphia's students are acquiring knowledge (through the use of standardized tests), activities deemed superfluous are abandoned.

The second possibility is very disturbing—in a remarkable, yet all too common, act of goal displacement, the aim of schools becomes passing tests, not the provision of a rich and meaningful education. Recalling that a commodity is something standard in unit and interchangeable by definition, it becomes quite easy to see how much of the knowledge gained in the service-learning experiment did not fit the conception of knowledge as a commodity, and hence, it became expendable.

Of course, there have been more recent instances of widespread marketization/privatization of schools and school systems. While too numerous to go into in detail, there is accumulating evidence that public schooling has been identified by market players (e.g., venture capitalists, hedge-fund managers, etc.) as an area ripe for exploitation (Schneider, 2016). The most infamous instance is probably post-Katrina New Orleans, of which Akers (2012) notes, "The introduction of charter schools and education vouchers has radically altered public education in the city by introducing market-based systems that require parents to act as consumers while exposing their children's future to the whims of the marketplace" (p. 29). Indeed, New Orleans's schools have been held up as a paradigmatic example of predatory disaster capitalism in both academic and popular presses (see, e.g., Kleing, 2007; Saltman, 2016).

The reduction of learning to simple metrics (e.g., test scores and dropout rates) in the wider context of market competition has also led to a number of cheating scandals, many involving teachers and/or administrators cheating to artificially raise test scores (Nichols & Berliner, 2007). From the "Texas Miracle" to the debacles in Washington, D.C., and Atlanta to countless more local transgressions, cheating scandals often co-occur with the rise of marketized competition. In the case of the Texas Miracle, President George W. Bush used Houston's remarkable test score rise as a justification for the rollout of the federal No Child Left Behind legislation. It was later determined that dropout rates were manipulated and potentially low-performing students in Houston were systemically prevented from even taking tests in an effort to artificially inflate district performance (Leung, 2004). The Washington, D.C., and Atlanta scandals resulted in scores of teachers being punished, often severely, for cheating (Shober, 2016). In both cases, the focus of the investigations and punishment was on teachers and not on the system that makes such behavior more likely.

These are just a few examples of the many possible ways in which market ideology's effect on knowledge conceptualization can impact schools. From the adoption of rigid curricula to gross overreliance on standardized tests, the belief that knowledge can be broken into easily measurable packages is already prevalent in public schools and the public conscience. These trends are due to an undergirding faith in markets as the solution to all social issues. Rethinking our metaphors about knowledge might offer a means to combat this commodifying paradigm.

Alternative Ways of Thinking and Doing: Makerspaces

We see makerspaces as a way to get beyond, or at least to combat, commodified versions of knowing. Makerspaces are the physical manifestation of the principles found in the maker movement that can take many forms: from a library with space designated for hands-on construction to a garage with sophisticated machinist tools. We have to admit, however, that we have a bit of a chicken–egg dilemma here. We see the promise of the maker movement and makerspaces as avenues that could interrupt how educational institutions quantify knowledge. But it is also true that for the maker movement and makerspaces to be established and for them to flourish, offering their full potential to students' constructive growth, we need flexible ways of non-market-based thinking to be prevalent. Our tack here is to suggest that finding opportunities to establish makerspaces in schools under the current commodifying paradigm can help begin to chip away at that paradigm. The very presence and use of makerspaces present an alternative narrative to that of the student as a commodity or a consumer of the commodities in school. In a makerspace, the student is a producer, a maker.

Simply establishing makerspaces in schools is not always an immediate option, so we also discuss how teachers can employ maker thinking to their existing classrooms and combat market thinking in small ways. In what follows, we describe the maker movement and suggest some makerspace-influenced practices in which teachers can engage that will provide students with non-commodified, organic, rich learning opportunities. Our hope is that students and teachers will be changed as a result of these experiences and that this will help with the chicken–egg problem. That is, these experiences will help loosen the grip that the business metaphor has on how they think about learning, and this will help make it possible for these sorts of experiences to proliferate.

The Maker Movement

Halverson and Sheridan (2014) define the maker movement as "the growing number of people who are engaged in the creative production of artifacts in their daily lives and who find physical and digital forums to share their processes and products with others" (p. 496). They describe the importance of the maker movement and its role in the changing landscape of education, highlighting how the maker movement involves the creation and sharing of artifacts while often employing digital technologies alongside the artifact. This is in line with constructivism, whereby the individual creates their knowledge through their actions in the world (Ackermann, 2001), as well as social constructivism as the individual is encouraged to seek out and create communities to co-create their knowledge (Vygotsky, 1978). These two elements alone are nothing new. However, where there is a delineation from other theories of learning is in the incorporation of construct*ion*ism, which encourages the individual to create an object (physical or digital) to showcase the knowledge they have gained in the world (Ackermann, 2001). All three learning theories put the student as the main agent of learning, while the teacher becomes the facilitator of knowledge, guiding the student to different repositories of knowledge. The maker movement is a combination of these three theories that allows for combating the market metaphor through the use of student-centered learning curricula. Thus, the maker movement is fundamentally social in nature.

However, there is also a tactile aspect of the maker movement requiring the use of not just digital tools but hand tools as well.

Makerspaces

Makerspaces are spaces that provide platforms for the work of the maker movement. They are the actualization of the conceptual movement and the associated definition. Many times, they are not large spaces but merely places for people to go and create. In short, makerspaces are not easily defined because they are created by different stakeholders (teachers, engineers, parents, etc.) within schools who want to offer the opportunity for students to create their own artifacts.

Makerspaces support independent work. These spaces typically have some technology in place within their realm that will allow people to create what they see fit. Most often, the spaces have computers with some sort of digital software to allow people to design whatever artifact they are interested in creating and then some sort of technology (three-dimensional [3D] printer, mechanical lathe, laser cutter, etc.) to actually create the artifact themselves. The environment is designed to encourage intellectual curiosity and interaction with different physical materials and social worlds. Ultimately, makerspaces take many forms, but they reflect the self-directed learner and allow people to feel as if they can engage different types of intelligence to explore the world in which they inhabit.

Makerspaces are places where people come together to learn through doing as a community. The spaces are designed to facilitate passionate inquiry into the interests of the student or group. Lave and Wenger (1991) define this type of community as "Communities of Practitioners" (p. 29). Lee and colleagues (2016) succinctly define Wenger's definition in the following statement: "Communities of practice are groups of people who share a concern or a passion for something they do and learn how to do it better as they interact regularly" ("Communities of Practice," para. 2). A real-world example of this has taken/is taking place at the Massachusetts

Institute of Technology, where it has created an assortment of community- and student-based makerspaces that allow people to come together to create. This idea, which is called Project Manus, is being replicated on university campuses around the world, not to mention in the local community. For example, Henrico County, Virginia libraries offer access to 3D printers, media labs, and other tools for the community to create. Not only do places like this exist and offer tools, but they also offer ways to learn those tools and build a community interested in similar ideas.

The vision makerspaces and the communities of practice promote can serve to trouble unexamined application of market metaphors about knowledge in several ways: (a) The application of the maker's mind to designing, troubleshooting, carrying out, and having a living artifact as a result of their work becomes a unified whole in the mind of the maker (and the teacher). The maker can certainly analyze that whole and talk about the components, but those components do not atomize into discrete skills that have objectified meaning outside of the total, holistic project. A skill or a concept used is not easily converted into a commodity. While any tradesperson has marketable skills, it is the application of those skills into immediate and real circumstances that gives them meaning and life, not the abstract possession of them that someone could demonstrate on a standardized exam. In short, making leads to a more grounded and correct view of what an idea is, what a skill is, and how, if they are to mean anything, it is in how we enact them in real life. (b) The product of making is more to the maker than its market value could ever represent. Attempting to render the product in terms of a market valuation feels like an insult to the total process by an engaged, thoughtful maker. While products are, of course, the stuff of economic exchange, and even the most experienced craftspeople live in the world where this has to be true, such makers always see those products as more than what was gotten from them in money, and the money almost never feels like compensation to the maker because the process was about the making, not about the money. The relationship between a person and what is supposed to be merely cold objects of exchange rendered by their labor gets reconfigured in truly engaged crafting and making. The grayscale pallet of the market world gets a technicolor infusion from understanding as a maker. (c) The competition of the market is de-emphasized in favor of cooperative exploration and problem-solving in communities of learning and practice.

The Draw of the Maker Movement

Why is the maker a current phenomenon in education and society? One way to understand it is that its growth comes out of a deficiency. The maker movement's popularity arises from the lack of the availability for people to work rather than merely to labor, to create rather than merely maintain, or just to tinker.

In school, the singular focus has become the acquiring of discrete abstractions as measurable skills or concepts. This does not even, as it purports to, prepare students for actual jobs requiring thinking but merely indoctrinates them into a world in which skills and concepts are mere tokens of exchange. There is the objectification of knowledge to the point where it becomes a commodity of value, the ultimate goal; the purity of the discrete abstraction creates an alienation from the ideas themselves. This creates a disconcerting feeling in the student. Students come to see thinking as unrelated to their lives outside of schools, which is also an unnatural, depressing state. Thinking is action, but only if it is used for the benefit of further thinking and enaction.

Similarly, Jackson (1971) states, "Adaptation to school life requires the student to become used to living under the constant condition of having their words and deeds evaluated by others" (p. 122). Students are discouraged from original thought because it becomes implicit in school that knowledge is a set of objects presented to them by others, measurable through standardized testing, and the only worthwhile information is that which will be tested.

The push to produce something that is not abstract but that is firmly planted in the physical world is the essence of the maker movement. It allows for knowledge workers to reassert their value as people who think non-abstractly, as makers through the creation of artifacts. Crawford's 2009 book *Shop Class as Soulcraft* is, in many ways, a long-form version of this argument. Crawford's book focuses on the larger subject of work, but he does have substantial ideas about the cognitive process that coincide with work and how important the production of artifacts has become with the over-valuing of abstract thought. Throughout his book, he compares the intellectual knowledge acquired through a book and the knowledge acquired through work. Crawford decries the educational system for upholding a fallible philosophy behind education while pointing to examples from his own life that reinforce his arguments against abstract knowledge. He goes so far as to undercut predictors of a commodified knowledge-based world in the statement "What is new is the wedding of futurism to what might be called 'virtualism': a vision of the future in which we somehow take leave of material reality and glide about in a pure information economy" (2009, p. 3). Crawford is concerned with the senseless uplifting of "pure knowledge" versus physical knowledge. Deriving one's knowledge from only the abstract thoughts confined in the mind can create a skewed idea about the surrounding world. Crawford describes a conversation with his physics professor father, during which they discuss the electrical components that are broken in a Volkswagen Beetle. The takeaway from this brief interaction is simple: The professor could intellectually explain the reason for the issue with the vehicle but lacked the real-world knowledge to help fix the issue. This story is related not to depict Crawford's father as an imbecile but rather to show how theoretical knowledge often cannot withstand practical application.

Crawford has succeeded within the intellectual realm: He has a doctorate in political philosophy from the University of Chicago, and he has written two books and numerous papers. However, he bemoans the demand for existing in one world, and he has personal experience for perspective as he is also a licensed electrician and mechanic. He sees a schism created by modernity between the mind and body, or the material world and the intellectual. He sees the tension in himself of being a lover of intellectuality and being a passionate mechanic. It is significant for him to be able to identify the crux of a problem with the way society uplifts the intellectual while debasing the physical in work and education due to his personal sharing of a life lived deeply in both worlds: material and intellectual. According to Crawford, "occupations based on universal, propositional knowledge are more prestigious, but they are also the kind that face competition from the whole world as book learning becomes more widely disseminated in the global economy" (2009, p. 162).

Makerspaces and Remaking Education Through Vocations

In Mike Rose's 2004 book *The Mind at Work*, he analyzes the connection between cognitive processes and working. Pertinent to this chapter, Rose's ideas about the relationship between the hand and brain both embody ideals of the maker movement and shed light on the creation of makerspaces. Rose argues for the importance of the connection between the hand and brain in trying to bridge the gap between academic and vocational education, or between thinking and doing. His ideas resonate deeply with the belief that there are multiple types of intelligence, and when we only teach in one manner, we fail to include, and even discourage, a large swath of students. Not only do we exclude students who may not grasp ideas in the presented manner, but students are also eliminated from a participatory culture that embodies the constructivist ideals within a classroom.

This reflects a correct understanding of the term *vocational education* in which *vocation*, from the same root as *evoke*, refers not to mere mechanical labor but to work of any kind as a calling. This was the sense in which Dewey (1929/2012) understood it in his strong advocacy for vocational education as a functional tool to enable students to become "fully realized" people. It supports the democratic principles he highlights throughout his philosophy of education. And it puts credence to the idea that students are the most important part of the learning equation: "The child's own instincts and powers furnish the material and give the starting-point for all education" (Dewey, 1929/2012, p. 33).

Dewey's version of vocational education sought to use work as a means toward the ends of personal and social growth. Dewey worried that conventional forms of vocational education provided overly specialized training. By readying an individual to complete one or a set of specialized tasks, it potentially lessened the likelihood of further growth by narrowing a student's perspectives and future possibilities. To Dewey, experiences that lead to future possible growth can be thought of as educative and those that lessen opportunities for growth should be thought of as miseducative. So a Deweyan vocational education involves using the learning about work to achieve both practical, traditional vocational ends and as a concrete foundation for learning that is more typically seen as the domain of a liberal education.

Dewey also prioritized the social dimensions of learning, and there are clear links between Dewey's thought and the contemporary social constructivist movement. Learning, to Dewey, is not an isolated affair but requires the interaction of people within a community to foster learning: "I believe all education proceeds by the participation of the individual in the social consciousness of the race" (1929/2012, p. 33). Even though there is often not the necessity for a community in a specific act of creating something, it is for the benefit of the learner to invite others into the process of making.

The Maker Movement and STEM/STEAM

Some are using the maker movement as a rallying point for stakeholders who are concerned about the science, technology, engineering, and math (STEM) learning in schools (Oliver, 2016). On the surface, this seems a viable way to combat the lack of interest and motivation of many students toward the STEM content areas. In reality, this situation presents both problems and opportunities. The primary problem is that STEM proponents all too often promote a hollow version of its content, focusing on individualistic and narrowly economic neoliberal versions of science and mathematics (Hytten & Stemhagen, 2019). The opportunity lies in the possibility to use STEM as a point of access for makerspaces. The hope is that once established, they will be able to help STEM to broaden its purpose and effects, reintegrating the STEM subject areas with the human dimensions of life and learning.

Hytten and Stemhagen (2019) argue that STEM and particularly the move from STEM to STEAM (STEM plus the arts) basically serves to reconstitute the curriculum minus the democratic/civic/human purposes of schooling. They argue that this does not need to be the case and that STEM can all be conceptualized in a way that embraces their human/social contexts. The presence of makerspaces in STEM programs can help students and teachers make such connections.

A practical example of reinvigorating the STEM subject areas can be found in the work of Litts et al. (2017). They describe a reimagined exploration and application of electricity through the use of conductive thread. This thread allowed students to weave LED lights and engage with some of the finer points of electricity while they created clothing that lit up and flashed different colors of LED lights. The project idea in itself was simple—allow students to create clothing with LED lights—but the applications and the underlying knowledge the students walked away from this project are indispensable to their formation of scientific knowledge. Moreover, the reason they were allowed to attempt such a feat is its connection to the STEM field.

Conclusion: The Hope and Possibility of Makerspaces

We have explained and critiqued the current tendency to see knowledge in market terms, that is, as a commodity, able to be abstracted from context, unitized, and measured, and we examined the role metaphor plays in our thinking about knowledge. Next, we suggested that certain social approaches have the promise of helping us see knowledge and its contexts as inextricably linked and that this linkage provides an important means to combat (often latent) commodified understandings of the nature of knowledge. We described, in some detail, the maker movement, positioning it as a potential practical approach to learning that embodies the social, context-focused conception of knowledge that we are advocating. In this conclusion, we very briefly consider how the maker movement might realistically fit into contemporary schooling.

Wilson and Gobeil (2017) provide one specific success story of makerspace implementation in schools. They created a makerspace for First Nations students to build guitars as a means to convey the standard curriculum. Their assumption was that a lack of connection to the curriculum (cultural incongruence) was partly to blame for low student engagement in the community. The makerspace included 3D design technology and computerized wood-milling technology, and students designed and built electric guitars. Their study showed increases in positive school experiences, increased engagement, and improved attendance. The authors suggest that the maker experience helped students to see curriculum as potentially relevant to their lives. One way to understand this change is that school knowledge, previously bound up in an abstract curriculum, was contextualized and freed of the restraints placed on it via its previous commodification.

The bulk of our argument about makerspaces operates at the level where school and society intersect, but teacher agency should be considered as well, as teachers are interacting with students and making daily decisions about the methods associated with the curriculum. In this chapter, we are not primarily concerned with specific curriculum and teaching methods that can be transformed or at least improved by including makerspaces, but prior to our final thoughts on the makerspace–school–society relationship, we want to articulate three specific sites for makerspaces in schools. We see the educational potential in schools for makerspaces to exist as standalone laboratories. In essence, they could become their own course work/content area. Second, as touched on earlier, we see great potential for makerspaces to be implemented in vocational education programs, specifically the ways in which technology and community are simultaneously featured. Third, there is promise for makerspaces to be created within traditional academic courses. In essence, makerspaces could be used to add relevance and application to the otherwise abstract academic curriculum.

One possible critique of this project is that one could argue that a non-commodified understanding of knowledge is needed to justify pedagogies like those suggested by the maker movement. In other words, makerspaces in schools are designed to help bring about the kind of society we'd like to see, yet they are more likely to happen if we have the kind of society likely to value them in the first place. Our answer to this critique is that our society is not monolithic, and while market metaphors undergird much of our thinking about phenomena not directly tied to commerce, markets, and so on, it is also true that we have other ways of thinking—while not currently preeminent in our culture—that have served as a counterbalance to market thinking. In the context of schooling, Labaree's (1997) account of the three purposes of schooling very nicely makes the case that in addition to two market-oriented purposes, social efficiency and social mobility, we have a long history in the United States of commitment to a third purpose, democratic equality. The maker movement, as we have characterized it, fits nicely with Labaree's third purpose. Labaree details how while, currently, market approaches are in the foreground, this social, human-focused purpose has never gone away and still has the potential to be more influential in educational policy and practice.

Prior to concluding, we want to briefly consider some more radical possibilities of the maker movement. What temperaments and sensibilities might the maker movement engender in students if they are introduced to it? Indeed, how might makerspaces affect the self-formation that can happen via schooling? We are enthused about the possibilities for children to become better equipped to be democratic participants, possessing an increased desire to participate in their social and political worlds. That is, the constructive aspects of becoming a maker can have real effects on student agency and on the desire for students to use their agency in the project of remaking their world as they learn to make things. There is also a question of whether a harder critical approach that tends to focus on the honing of students' faculties to recognize and remedy structural inequality is too convergent on adults' sense of what needs to be fixed and, as a result, might not always be the best path toward the cultivation of genuine agency. We see makerspaces as a possible way to foster agency without the indoctrinaire undertones of some explicitly critical projects. Makerspaces have the potential to be more agentic than mainstream democratic approaches while also an indirect (non-indoctrinaire) way to work against commodification.

Finally, in addition to the presence of possibility within the institution of public school, one can also see in our non-monolithic society, some promising trends. The maker movement can be seen as existing within broader cultural veins of attention to craft and a return to the benefits of respect for human scale in creating the world in which we live. When thought of in this way, one can see that there is hope that the maker movement and other humanizing pedagogies will be able to find an increased place in schools and that their presence holds promise to help students experience knowledge in non-commodified ways.

Notes

1. We first articulated the claim that a general market mentality has led to a commodification of knowledge and that this is problematic at the 2004 South Atlantic Philosophy of Education Society meeting (Stemhagen, 2005).

References

Ackermann, E. (2001). Piaget's constructivism, Papert's constructionism: What's the difference? *Future of Learning Group Publication, 5*(3), 1–11.

Akers, J. (2012). Separate and unequal: The consumption of public education in post-Katrina New Orleans. *International Journal of Urban and Regional Research, 36*(1), 29–48.

Stemhagen, K. (2005). Market metaphors and the commodification of knowledge. In J. McKernan (Ed.), *South Atlantic philosophy of education 2004 yearbook,* South Atlantic Philosophy of Education Society (pp. 88–102).

Caruso, D. (2004, June 23). Philly's schools get mixed results: Test scores rise despite high dropout rates, unsafe environment. *Houston Chronicle.*

Crawford, M. B. (2009). *Shop class as soulcraft:An inquiry into the value of work.* Penguin Press.

Dewey, J. (2012). My pedagogic creed. In D. J. Flinders & S. J. Thornton (Eds.), *The curriculum studies reader* (4th ed., pp. 33–40). Taylor & Francis. (Original work published 1929)

Freire, P. (2000). *Pedagogy of the oppressed.* Continuum International Publishing Group.

Halverson, E., & Sheridan, K. (2014). The maker movement in education. *Harvard Educational Review, 84*(4), 495–504.

Hornbeck, D. (2000). Service-learning and reform in the Philadelphia public schools. *Phi Delta Kappan, 81*(9), 665.

Hytten, K., & Stemhagen, K. (2019). When STEM and STEAM really mean ABC: A democratic critique of "anything but civics" schools. *Educational Studies, 56*(1), 18–36.

Jackson, P. (1971). The daily grind. In D. J. Flinders & S. J. Thornton (Eds.), *The curriculum studies reader* (4th ed., pp. 117–127). Taylor & Francis.

Klein, N. (2007, October). Disaster capitalism: The new economy of catastrophe. *Harper's Magazine,* pp. 47–58.

Labaree, D. F. (1997). Public goods, private goods: The American struggle over educational goals. *American Education Research Journal, 34*(1), 39–81.

Lave, J., & Wenger, E. (1991). *Situated learning: legitimate peripheral participation.* Cambridge University Press.

Lee, J., Ng, J., Rabinovich, A., & Wu, J. (2016, November 23). *Communities of practice.* https://www.learning-theories.com/communities-of-practice-lave-and-wenger.html

Leung, R. (2004, January 6). The "Texas miracle" (Season 6, episode 14) [TV episode]. In *60 minutes II.* CBS. https://www.cbsnews.com/news/the-texas-miracle

Litts, B., Kafai, Y., Lui, D., Walker, J., & Widman, S. (2017). Stitching codeable circuits: High school students' learning about circuitry and coding with electronic textiles. *Journal of Science Education and Technology, 26*(5), 494–507.s

Nichols, S., & Berliner, D. (2007). *Collateral damage: How high-stakes testing corrupts America's schools*. Harvard Education Press.

Oliver, K. M. (2016). Professional development considerations for makerspace leaders, part one: Addressing "What?" and "Why?" *TechTrends, 60*(3), 160–166.

Rose, M. (2004). *The mind at work*. Viking Penguin.

Saltman, K. (2016). *Capitalizing on disaster: Taking and breaking public schools*. Routledge.

Schneider, M. (2016). *School choice: The end of public education?* Teacher College Press.

Shober, A. (2016). *In common no more: The politics of the Common Core State Standards*. Praeger.

Vygotsky, L. S. (1978). *Mind in society*. Harvard University Press.

Wilson, J., & Gobeil, M. (2017). Guitars and makerspace: Examining the experience of First Nations students. *Canadian Journal of Learning and Technology, 43*(2), 1–16.

Chapter Seven

UNIONIZING EDUCATORS IN CHARTER SCHOOLS:

A CASE STUDY OF THE CHICAGO TEACHER'S UNION ORGANIZING MODEL

by Michelle Strater Gunderson

I woke up extra early on a December morning in 2018, put on my red down coat, and headed out to a picket line in Chicago. The sign I was carrying said "Love Charter Educators—Loathe Charter Operators." That was the morning of the first strike in our country against a charter organization. The Acero charter system is one of the largest in Chicago, serving more than 7,000 students. The educators in these buildings were ready to take a stand against overcrowded classes, low wages, and insufficient supports for bilingual students and children with special needs (Jones, 2018). Many of us walking the frigid picket line that morning had a feeling that we were participating in a historic event. It was the fruition of years of organizing work.

This chapter is a case study of the Chicago Teachers Union's (CTU's) campaign to organize charter school educators into our union. As a member of the CTU executive board and an activist leader in Chicago, I am fully embedded in this work, and this case study is greatly influenced by my personal involvement. Whenever possible, I give firsthand accounts of occasions taken from my notes. In addition, the findings of this study are based on 10 in-depth interviews with key teacher leaders and organizers of the charter campaign, as well as notes from meetings, internal emails, and publications.

Five themes emerged in the study: (1) building a theory of the case for charter unionization, (2) establishing unions from the ground up, (3) shifting cultures and consciousness, (4) overcoming fear, (5) and lessons learned. The final draft of this chapter was reviewed by three members of the CTU charter school division to check for accuracy and concurrence. Let me note that the voices of individual teachers outside of the leadership team were not included in this short work. A broader view from a larger study is warranted to check for historical repercussions and the impact of this organizing effort on a wide range of teacher practitioners.

I hope that a clear example of a successful campaign against the privatization and commodification of public education will serve as a guide for others even when approaching an issue other than charter schools. As educators, we are not powerless in confronting the forces that commodify and narrow the focus of our work.

Theory Of The Case

The creation of a charter school union in Chicago started as a joint project between the Illinois Federation of Teachers, the American Federation of Teachers, and the CTU. It was simply called "The Charter Project." The CTU began to aggressively organize charter unions when the leadership changed in 2010.

The CTU is currently run by leadership from the Caucus of Rank and File Educators (CORE). A group of concerned educators formed this union caucus to fight the impending schooling reforms that sought to privatize public education and reduce the power of collective bargaining agreements and teachers' unions. Members of CORE found themselves in the middle of huge reforms in the Chicago schools. There was an increase in high-stakes testing of students, the curriculum we were forced to teach became increasingly narrow, and our neighborhood schools were at risk of closing partly due to the proliferation of charter schools in the city. It is as if Chicago teachers were personally living the commodification reforms mentioned throughout this book.

A key component of the guiding principles of CORE is upholding the right of our community to keep our schools in the hands of the public (CORE, 2020). The concept of charter schools, putting public money in the hands of private enterprises to run schools, is in direct opposition to CORE's principles. Once in leadership CORE educators changed the CTU from a business model, one whereby the union takes care of pay and benefits, to a social justice–oriented union that is just as concerned with the broader political and community concerns as it is with teachers' job conditions (Weiner, 2012). This shift in leadership focus is important for understanding the driving motivation behind unionizing charter schools in the city.

Throughout the early 2000s, Chicago saw an unprecedented increase in charter schools. As of 2016, 22% of Chicago Public Schools (CPS) students in Grades 9 through 12 were enrolled in a charter high school, compared to only 4% a decade earlier (Gwynne & Moore, 2017). These schools are run by private corporations and nonprofit groups that do not have to follow the same standards as the public schools in the city. In addition, they generate added levels of bureaucracy to support the public–private contracts. As a result, there is a diminished accountability to the public even though the schools are funded with tax dollars. In essence, public money that should have been allocated to public schools gets shifted to private school corporations operating under conditions not vetted by the public.

Because charter schools are funded through a per student formula, charter schools actively recruit students from existing schools, thus destabilizing the student enrollment in neighborhood public schools (Lutton et al., 2018). The leaders of the CTU realized that we needed to eradicate the incentive to have charter operators to turn our city's children into objects—commodities representing their profit. A dynamic that is of specific concern to the CTU is how often the charter school recruitment appealed to the racial divisions in the city (Lamberti, 2014).

Another concern of the union is that the educators in charter schools receive lower salaries when compared to teachers in district-run public schools (Jones, 2018). For example, teachers in Chicago's Noble Charter Schools made on average $52,000 a year in 2016, compared to an average salary of $74,000 in district-run schools. One of the goals of the charter teacher strikes in 2018–2019 was to shrink the gap between charter and district teachers' salaries. According to Chris Baehrend, the president of the CTU charter division,

> the savings from lower teacher salaries seldom make it to providing better resources to the classroom. Our analysis of charter school budgets shows that it overwhelmingly results in a layer of well-paid school administrative staff, adding to the bureaucracy of the system.

Charter schools were also seen as a threat to collective bargaining, the ability to negotiate a contract effectively, for district teachers. Having a large section of workers in our schools who were not unionized would diminish the ability to mobilize workers into a strike action. For example, during the CTU strike of 2012, charter organizations actively recruited and advertised for students. The charter schools were hoping to increase their student enrollment, and, in so doing, weakened the positions of the public school teachers who were striking to negotiate a contract for better working and learning conditions. If families had left the public schools for the charter schools, it would have greatly weakened the teachers' union political position. Thankfully, this did not happen.

In the end, the CTU decided to commit considerable energy and funding into unionizing charter school educators. "We needed to slow down the speeding train where charter schools were overrunning our public school systems, like they did in New Orleans," says Jackson Potter, then chief of staff of the Chicago Teachers Union. "There was a clear need to have a workable strategy to offset the control charter organizations were having over our district because from national experience it was clear they were not going away."

Shifting Culture And Consciousness

One of the biggest obstacles to overcome when working with charter schools is the business model concept of running schools. In the business model, educators are praised and rewarded as laborers whose value consists in emerging with a quality product; for the most part, this means increased student test scores. The individual laborer who makes the finished product most efficiently gets rewarded, while the individual laborer who does not gets condemned and eventually fired. This view objectifies students as products and teachers as interchangeable labor units.

The charter teachers interviewed for this chapter talked about feeling like a cog in a wheel—that the relationship to the charter system was mechanical rather than a human relationship between student and teacher. Teacher Chris Baehrend talks about how he felt pressured into being a "testing machine." He states,

> I was eager to provide my students with an engaging curriculum. To make a difference. But the focus was constantly on the test scores. When I was working at Latino Youth High School in 2009 I had no textbooks, no computers, the copier was broken. I kept saying to myself "this is not the school the kids deserve."

He went on to explain that he felt his worth as a teacher was being judged by how his students performed on standardized tests rather than the quality of the teaching and learning. He also saw teachers fired summarily when the administration viewed them as underperforming, yet they were given little support or resources.

From the teachers' point of view, the business model means that for them to succeed, they have to strictly perform as successful individual laborers and to eschew other individual laborers who are not as successful. Another, seemingly paradoxical, facet of the business model is that the successful laborer-teacher in this environment is also configured as a savior to the students and the minority community. Both of these elements promote a teacher identity toxic in its individualism.

Mihir Garaud was a charter school educator in Philadelphia when he saw the movie *Waiting for "Superman"* (Guggenheim et al., 2010). "In this movie the teachers are seen as the source of the problem," says Garaud.

> I think I internalized this and believed it for a while. That the problem was individual teachers who did not care about kids. I did not point to the system as being wrong. When I came to Chicago in 2015, I saw people coming together over the same issues—student learning, school conditions, and resources—but the teachers were working together to solve the problems rather than working as individuals. This was my introduction to the Chicago Teachers Union.

When building a union consciousness, the culture of a school needs to shift from individual success to collective work and support. Excessive individualism is an impediment to working cooperatively and collectively to form a union and the competition between teachers isolates us from each other.

Understanding The Function Of A Teacher Union

A large first step in this organizing was helping educators understand the function of a union. Labor unions have experienced such a steady decline over the last half of the 20th century that many new teachers have no direct exposure to union structures and the need to build rights and responsibilities in the workplace. Jen Conant, one of the teacher leaders who organized her charter school, talks about the need to educate teachers about unions in general:

> Many teachers had been exposed to a decades-long media coverage of painting unions as the enemy. Unions were often cast as the barriers to "good education" for students. Teachers that I was talking with had negative views that needed to be talked through.

One of the ways that administrators and bosses try to portray the union as the enemy is by using a tactic called "third partying." In essence, the administration tries to characterize the union as an outside force that does not have the teachers' and students' interests at heart. They often argue that the members will not have a voice and that they will have to succumb to the power of the union. Charter school administrators would say, "Why would you pay a third party to speak for you when our school is such a great place to work?" according to Chris Baehrend. At first, this argument might seem reasonable to teachers, but pointing out the advantages of working collectively for working conditions and job protections usually won out. Educators at charter schools many times had stories relating to extensive amounts of extra work placed on teachers as well as unfair treatment, yet any time they spoke up they were threatened with being fired.

While passing out union flyers at a charter school during an organizing campaign, Mihir Garud says a group of teachers told him, "We don't need a union. We can solve all of our problems with our principal." This was more than likely true; there are hardworking and sincere educators who administrate charter schools. But the reality is that bosses never remain constant and that workers need protections over their teaching and learning conditions.

Another problem union organizers faced was the power dynamic between charter bosses and school employees. Many charter teachers are at the beginning of their careers and are much younger than district faculties. New teachers are often in vulnerable positions in terms of tenure, and in many charter contracts, the teachers are considered "at will" employees, meaning they can be fired without cause. Chris Baehrend states, "It is amazing how much trust teachers put into their bosses. The charter school ethos is built on innovation and supposed teacher freedom. Many teachers believed that charter schools had saved them from working in bad places." Yet the facts tell a different story. The retention rate for Chicago charter teachers in 2016 was 63% compared to the overall retention rate of district teachers at 83% (Sanchez, 2016). "It is heartbreaking to organize with charter educators and see so many people walk out the revolving door," added Baehrend.

Because of this power dynamic, teachers interviewed said they experienced being "talked down to" by the bosses, especially in terms of their ability to understand school financing. Charter school organizer Casey Sweeney identifies this as part of the patriarchal structure of some charter schools. One teacher called it the "why worry your pretty little head" syndrome. In essence, there is an attitude that the people in charge of the school know what is right for the workers. Sweeney recommends that teachers become experts regarding their school's budget and finances, not only learning to contradict statements made by operators but also helping teachers identify waste and, at times, misspending of funds.

The financial argument that charter operators often make is that a union contract with higher wages will impact the staffing numbers in a school. They threaten that the school will experience drastic staffing cuts if the union contract terms are met. As Chris Baehrend states, "this argument often works because teachers by nature are caring people, and this appeals to their need to take care of others."

Other obstacles in educating teachers about unions are the anti-union campaigns held by the charter operators. Once a union organizing campaign starts, educators are often called into what Norine Gutekanst calls a "captive audience presentation." In several instances, attorneys and outside professional organizations were used to build formal antiunion campaigns. Mihir Garud remembers a meeting during which the educators were gathered in an auditorium for an antiunion campaign presented by an outside professional organization. "In other words," Garud says, "local tax dollars meant to educate children are being used to deny workers the federal right to organize. Money that should go directly to the classrooms."

Casey Sweeney recalls one administrator during a "captive audience" meeting saying, "I wish I could speak to you from my heart, but I have to read these prepared remarks from our legal consultants." This is one of the ways that "us against them" polarization takes place, often painting the union as the "bad guys."

In every instance of pushback from the administrators of charter school operations, union organizers have to shift the conversation away from individualism to a sense of collective work, as well as overcoming the negative narrative many charter teachers hear about unions.

Union Organizing From The Ground Up

The first premise of any good organizing model is to find common ground with the people you want to mobilize. The CTU held many meetings with charter school educators. At these meetings, organizers emphasized student needs and our ability to advocate for what they needed. According to Norine Gutekanst, this approach "resounded with teachers because they did want to improve children's lives." In fact, a major issue in the charter school strikes during the 2018–2019 school years was the lack of resources and personnel, such as psychologists and social workers, for children with special needs (Wong & Escobar, 2018).

'We have two ears and one mouth for a reason' is a tried and true union precept. Through these listening sessions, school leaders and organizers are able to find common ground and unifying issues. Says Casey Sweeney,

> We found that many teachers were able to identify the lower pay and working conditions as key points of agreement. Charter teachers would say, "All they want is more and more." Teachers were working under conditions that could not be sustained and they saw a revolving door of teacher turnover at their school sites.

As a result of the meetings, the CTU decided to create the Chicago Teachers Union Alliance of Charter Teachers and Staff (CTU-ACTS). The group distilled a set of common concerns that they felt most charter educators shared and used these concerns to build their organizing campaign:

1. Providing high-quality education to all children
2. Strengthening the teaching profession
3. Improving teaching and learning conditions
4. Creating a mechanism for teacher voice in school decision-making

Organizers stress how each charter school context has its own unique culture, yet there seems to be a regular pattern that emerges in most of the campaigns. The first is to identify leaders in the school interested in union organizing. Once leaders are identified, training and building communications skills begin. Casey Sweeney says, "It is important that every step of the organizing process is member driven, not staff driven." Sweeney emphasized that the workers in the building set the pace and tone of the interactions.

It is advised that these initial meetings take place in secret. All the union organizers in their interviews stressed how important it is to keep educators' activism and organizing status confidential until a large-enough group was formed. This helps lessen the possibility of management coming after particular leaders with no one else there to back them up. It is best to wait for a large percentage of the building to agree to join the union before starting any public campaigns.

After the initial committee is formed it is time to "map the building." This is a strategy where leaders decide which relationships in the building exist and who can be influential. A detailed description of this process can be found in *Secrets of a Successful Organizer* (Bradbury et al., 2016) published by Labor Notes, but in essence, mapping the building means analyzing the power dynamics in a workplace and discovering relationships.

Next, the CTU organizers and member leaders all agree that it is time to start having organizing conversations. These conversations are called "one on ones" for a reason—it is essential they take place in person. It is easier to address obstacles and form shared understandings when talking with a person face-to-face. "Honest conversations with individuals are the only way to organize this work," says Casey Sweeney.

Once relationships have been established and organizing conversations have commenced, it is time to build a series of actions.. The process of organizing is organic, but there is a menu of certain steps that almost all charter campaigns go through. Some of the actions include asking teachers to wear union shirts 1 day a week, asking teachers to sign an "intent to commit" card with the understanding that it will not be made public unless a 70% threshold is reached, or passing out flyers outside of the building to garner community support.

As organizers, we are constantly reminding ourselves that the relationships with fellow unionists are ongoing. In other words, one conversation is never enough. At each step of the way, union leaders are asking for verbal support and checking in with how members are feeling as well as what they are thinking. Casey Sweeney says, "For anyone doing this work this most important thing to remember is that you constantly reassess what you are doing and why, and analyze the effectiveness of the activities."

After large organizing efforts behind the scenes, it was time to convince educators to sign a union card. In each building, the leaders had to create a collective consciousness and confidence to bring enough people on board to create critical mass. Mihir Garud, an officer with the charter division, says, "Time and trust are essential in this work. People's livelihoods are at stake . . . and the stakes are high."

Overcoming Fear

The organizing leaders of the CTU-ACTS campaign realized that fear would be one of the biggest obstacles to overcome when convincing charter educators to organize. One of the first items they published was a "know your rights" document (see https://www.ctulocal1.org/wp-content/uploads/2018/09/Your-Right-to-Organize.docx). In this document, the union listed the legal basis for organizing union members in a school, including a list of possible retaliation tactics an employer might use. The charter union organizers interviewed for this case study universally identify misinformation and legal intimidation as two common themes in their organizing context. One organizer stated, "The laws themselves don't keep the bosses from breaking them. We have to constantly be watching for dirty pool."

To help educators new to union organizing, it is standard practice to inoculate the workers against difficulties they might face. Inoculation is a time-honored organizing precept in labor unions. It is a way of helping potential union members predict the obstacles they might face so that they can overcome the roadblocks they will eventually face. Organizers need to make sure that risks are explained fully.

One way of inoculating workers to opposition is to anticipate tactics that management might tack and develop role-playing scenarios so that teachers build confidence in their ability to respond to opposition. In one organizing campaign, the committee leaders made inoculation bingo cards of all the phrases they predicted management would use. It was a lighthearted and effective way to communicate, and many of the bingo cards were full by the end of the campaign. Casey Sweeney says inoculation is "giving the educators a little taste of what they are up against in order to lessen the impact. An organizer needs to be really upfront about the things that can go wrong."

Some of the management tactics that organizers list are (a) increasing surveillance and pop-in observations, (b) making an example of someone by giving them a difficult schedule or new assignment, (c) enforce rules unevenly giving special treatment to teachers who are not in favor of the union, or (d) threatening to close a school site.

All the persons interviewed for this study mention trust as a key factor in overcoming fear. Jen Conant says, "Building trusting relationships is everything in this work. You cannot make change without trust, and organizing is not difficult when you genuinely care about the relationships." Helping new unionists anticipate the struggles they might have to overcome builds trust because workers can see that the union organizers have been frank and truthful regarding the difficulties inherent in organizing.

Norine Gutekanst stated that "CTU built its reputation during the 2012 teachers strike. Teachers in the charter schools saw us as fighters for students. We overcame the narrative of the greedy, lazy teacher because our strike was about better learning conditions for students." Gutekanst believes that our fight for students gained credibility and gained people's trust.

Lessons Learned

"If I were to choose one mistake that impacted my organizing, it would be that I tried to do too much myself," says Mihir Garud. He went on to talk about the importance of mapping a building, knowing and understanding the relationships workers have with each other, and using those relationships to build trust. One piece of advice that Garud would give others organizing charter schools is that you have to identify and develop the well-respected leaders in the school. "None of this work can be done alone," he says.

Another aspect of charter school organizing that Casey Sweeney says needs to be openly addressed is how much founding charter teachers, those who started the school, deeply identify with the mission of the charter. One of the tactics an administration will take to hamper a union campaign is to polarize the teaching force, pitting one teacher against another. Forming wedges between the teachers who started a building from the ground up and those new to the school is common.

For example, one charter school director held a brunch for the founding teacher leaders of the school. The director used the opportunity to explain how the union would ruin the school they had worked to build together: "We should have prepared these teachers for how personal this would be."

One of the teachers who attended this brunch related to Casey Sweeney that even though she was ready for attacks from the administration it still was emotionally painful. "She said that having all the work and time she poured into building the school questioned hurt deeply." Listening to this teacher helped Sweeney realize the importance of working with the founding teachers and addressing their personal commitment to the school along with the highly emotional attachment the teachers have to the vision of the school.

Jen Conant relates the importance of including as many workers as possible in the union organizing. She recalls when the group of paraprofessional staff wanted to unionize and demanded recognition. One of the ways that administrators divide workers is by separating different job categories from each other within a building. "It is powerful that they would take that risk collectively," says Conant. At the end of the interview, Conant stated, "Change is hard, but it's worth it. Our students are worth it. We are worth it."

Conclusion

Every organizing context is different and complex, but there are certain precepts to labor organizing that the CTU used that can be generalizable to campaigns for fighting the privatization of education and the subsequent diminishing of schooling as a public good.

Organize from the ground up, follow the lead of the teacher leaders in the schools, address the importance of unions in improving the lives of teachers and students, and develop a sense of solidarity. Charter schools are part of the commodification and privatization trend in American education, and pushing back against this one factor is part of resisting the concept as a whole.

"People who go through the process of unionizing become so changed by it. It can be transformational. It is the first time for many people to experience challenging power. They will never be the same," says Casey Sweeney.

Recommended Further Reading

Bradbury, A., Brenner, M., Brown, J., Slaughter, J., & Winslow, S. (2015). *How to jumpstart your union: Lessons from the Chicago teachers.* Labor Notes.

Charney, M., Hagopian, J., & Peterson, R. (Eds.). (2020). *Teachers unions and social justice: Organizing for the schools and communities our students deserve.* Rethinking Schools.

References

Bradbury, A., Brenner, M., & Slaughter, J. (2016). *Secrets of a successful organizer.* Labor Notes.

Caucus of Rank and File Educators. (2020). *CORE by-laws.* https://www.coreteachers.org/core_by_laws

Guggenheim, D. (Producer/Writer), Chilcott, L. (Producer), & Kimball, B. (Writer). (2010). *Waiting for "Superman"* [Film]. Walden Media.

Gwynne, J. A., & Moore, P. T. (2017). *Chicago's charter schools: Organizational features, enrollment, school transfers, and school performance.* University of Chicago Consortium on School Research. https://charterschoolcenter.ed.gov/sites/default/files/files/field_publication_attachment/Chicagos%20Charter%20High%20Schools-Nov2017-Consortium.pdf

Jones, S. (2018, December). Inside the nation's first charter school strike; '30K is not a livable wage in Chicago.' *New York Magazine*. https://nymag.com/intelligencer/2018/12/inside-acero-teacher-strike.html

Lamberti, C. (2014, March 1). *Selling choice: Marketing charter schools in Chicago*. Chicago Teachers Union. https://www.ctulocal1.org/wp-content/uploads/2018/10/Selling-Choice-Marketing-Charter-Schools-in-Chicago.pdf

Lutton, L., Vevea, B., Karp, S., Cardon-Magnigad, A., & McGee, K. (2018, December 8). *A generation of school closings*. WBEZ. https://interactive.wbez.org/generation-school-closings/

Sanchez, M. (2016, February 8). *Autonomy at any price*. The Chicago Reporter. https://www.chicagoreporter.com/autonomy-at-a-price/

Weiner, L. (2012). *The future of our schools: Teachers unions and social justice*. Haymarket.

Wong, A., & Escobar, N. (2018, December). The charter-school teachers' strike in Chicago was "inevitable." *The Atlantic*. https://www.theatlantic.com/education/archive/2018/12/charter-school-strike-chicago/577459/

Chapter Eight

WHAT ARE "SOFT SKILLS," AND SHOULD WE BE TEACHING THEM?

by Bailey B. Smolarek

The term *soft skills* has emerged as one of the most prominent educational discourses of the 21st century. Sometimes referred to as "noncognitive skills" or "21st-century skills," soft skills are considered interpersonal dispositions and transferable personality traits. Soft skills differ from their "hard" skills counterpart in that hard skills refer to specific abilities and knowledge required to do a particular job or task (e.g., web design, foreign language proficiency) whereas soft skills refer to more general abilities such as communication, creativity, teamwork, and critical thinking (Gallivan et al., 2004; Hora et al., 2016).

Recent changes to the labor market, such as deindustrialization, the growth of the knowledge economy, and decreased job stability, have led to a considerable push for more soft-skills training to create flexible employees with transferable skills (Deming, 2017; Heckman & Kautz, 2012). Proponents contend that desirable soft skills lead to labor market and school advancement, decreased criminal conduct, improved marriage outcomes, and general "success in life" (Duckworth et al., 2007; Heckman & Rubenstein, 2001). This emerging body of literature has prompted econometricians (Deming, 2017; Heckman & Kautz, 2012) and a subset of psychologists (Duckworth et al., 2007) to pursue the standardization of soft skills to cultivate more desirable employees and promote labor market productivity. This has led to research attempting to provide precise definitions, taxonomies, and measurements for these skills.

Yet it is important to notice how the dominant soft skills discourse is based on a very particular vision of soft skills that evaluates one's personality and/or personal attributes through predominantly human capital measures of success (i.e., income earnings, employment status, criminal record; Duckworth et. al, 2007; Heckman & Rubenstein, 2001). This approach views desirable soft skills as decontextualized traits favored by the free market and subsequently operationalizes and assesses such traits based on their potential economic return. Such an approach dehumanizes students by reducing them to commodities to be bought and sold on the labor market as future employees (Choo, 2018; Gershon, 2011; Urciuoli, 2008; Walkerdine, 2005).

This chapter contests the homogenizing and commodifying nature of the soft skills discourse by examining the idea as a historical and morally laden construct and providing alternative viewpoints and understandings. Through the lens of cultural capital (Bourdieu, 1986; Bourdieu & Passeron, 1977; Yosso, 2005), I present qualitative interview data with a predominantly female (94%) group of nursing educators and students. When the former and future nurses who participated in this study were asked about the skills, competencies, knowledge, and abilities they believed nurses need most, their answers defied prevailing conceptualizations of soft skills that emphasize productivity and profit. Instead, participants highlighted the importance of ideas related to caring, love, compassion, and advocacy that are rarely (if ever) included in the broader soft-skill discussions and measurements.

Analysis of their responses adds to our understanding of soft skills in "caring professions" (e.g., nursing, teaching, childcare work, social work) by promoting a more socially just and culturally centered understanding. While the prevailing soft skills discourse renders the idea of caring as something to be done for material gain, the nursing participants discussed in the chapter do not consider the care they provide to their patients and patients' loved ones something they do for profit. Rather, the care they provide is something they are compelled to do from a heartfelt, ethical, and moral position. This motivation, and the rationales provided by nursing participants, is applicable to not only nursing education but also to the training and practice of other caring professions, such as teaching. I argue that female-dominated caring professions, like the nurses discussed in this chapter, provide a compelling and often-overlooked understanding of soft skills that challenges the current discourse's commodifying nature.

Emergence of the Soft-Skills Discourse

The first documented usage of the term *soft skills* is attributed to educator L. Steven Zwerling's 1976 book *Second Best: The Crisis of the Community College*, which argues that community colleges maintain inequality and reproduce social-class hierarchies by relying solely on vocational education and utilizing tactics to lower student aspirations. Zwerling reasons that community colleges must help students cultivate soft skills to facilitate upward social mobility. This discussion primarily includes an assortment of coping and adjustment mechanisms to better prepare predominantly low-income students for the culture shock they experience upon transferring to a 4-year college. Zwerling focuses his argument on disrupting the social class reproduction process by preparing students to interact with the "bourgeois" through soft skills education.

When Zwerling first discussed the teaching of soft skills, he did so in support of a larger argument concerning the role of schooling in social reproduction. However, since that time, the term *soft skills* has been primarily used in econometric analyses to promote human capital development (Heckman & Katuz, 2012; Heckman & Rubinstein, 2001). The following section defines these two competing frameworks for soft skills (social reproduction vs. human capital) by tying them to their theoretical underpinnings and exploring their empirical validity.

Soft Skills as a Mechanism of Social and Cultural Reproduction

At the time Zwerling's (1976) book was published, there was a burgeoning field of neo-Marxist scholarship examining the reproduction of social inequalities through schooling (Apple, 1982; Giroux, 1981). Perhaps the most seminal text on topic, Bowles and Gintis's *Schooling in Capitalist America* (also published in 1976) offered a neo-Marxist analysis that posited a corresponding relationship between schooling and the capitalist labor market. Bowles and Gintis concluded that social relationships within schools (i.e., relationships between teachers and students, students and students, and teachers and administrators) replicate and reify the hierarchical divisions of labor in U.S. capitalism. Although they did not use the specific term *soft skills*, Bowles and Gintis discussed ideas commonly associated with soft skills in determining labor market outcomes and/or economic prosperity. Specifically, Bowles and Gintis argued that factors impacted by social class, such as socialization and educational opportunities, predict future economic success more aptly than "cognitive requirements" (1976, p. 47). In other words, regardless of how smart a person is, social class (coupled with its associated dispositions and societal dis/advantages) more often determines a person's socioeconomic outcome.

Where Bowles and Gintis (1976) and other theories of socio-economic reproduction left off, theories of cultural reproduction have advanced by examining the role of culture and cultural transmission within social class domination. Most notably, Bourdieu and Passeron (1977) assert that schools do not necessarily mirror labor market structures but rather reward students who possess particular cultural characteristics (or soft skills) associated with the middle and upper classes. They term these characteristics "cultural capital"—which they divide into three subforms: "objectified" (e.g., books, musical instruments), "institutionalized" (e.g., degrees, legal qualifications), and "embodied" (e.g., language, manners). Over time, Bourdieu and Passeron (1977) argue, embodied forms of cultural capital are impressed upon a person's "habitus," meaning a person's intellectual and embodied disposition, to convey social class through embodied gestures, such as how a person walks, talks, eats, sits, laughs, or smiles. Schooling participates in the social reproduction process by promoting and legitimizing dominant class forms of cultural capital, rewarding students who possess these forms and imposing them on students who do not.

Bourdieu and Passeron (1977) refer to the imposition of dominant forms of cultural capital on those who are in positions of being dominated as "symbolic violence." This type of violence denies the legitimacy of worth based on culture and reflects a general understanding of students from nondominant cultures as deficits who disproportionately "fail" because of their perceived lack of ability and/or aspirations (Conchas, 2006; Steele, 1997; Valenzuela, 1999). Scholars have discredited cultural deficit models and instead demonstrated the need to examine institutional barriers and sociopolitical factors that affect school practices and relationships (Anyon, 1997; Delgado Gaitán, 2001). Moreover, educational scholars have asserted the need to recognize and embrace forms of cultural capital present in nondominant communities (e.g., low-income communities and communities of color) to better serve these populations (Gay, 2000; Gonzáles et al., 2005, Ladson-Billings, 1995). Tara Yosso (2005), for example, asked the fundamental question of "whose culture has capital" by examining the often overlooked "community cultural wealth" that poor students and students of color bring to school. Yosso argues that "cultural capital is not just inherited or possessed by the middle class, but rather it refers to an accumulation of specific forms of knowledge, skills, and abilities that are valued by privileged groups in society" (2005, p. 76).

While the literature on cultural capital directly speaks to the current discursive understandings of soft skills as transferable personality traits and interpersonal dispositions, discussions of social reproduction, class bias, and cultural capital are rarely included in soft skill debates that are almost always dominated by econometric analyses that use a human capital lens.

Soft Skills as a Means of Human Capital Development

Largely at odds with cultural capital theory, human capital theory was developed in the 1960s as an economic theory of labor wherein investments in education, health, and people are evaluated by their potential future economic benefits (Becker, 1983; Schultz, 1961). Through the lens of human capital theory, education is viewed as a commodity to be bought and sold and is evaluated almost exclusively on individual incomes or earnings. This lens assumes a very particular desired result (i.e., a high salary) that can significantly limit the ways in which educational objectives are conceptualized. Nevertheless, human capital analyses in education research have become ubiquitous (Spring, 2015), influencing everything from literacy (Bartlett, 2007) to girls' education (Moeller, 2018) to teacher training (Buras, 2011). When soft skills are analyzed through a human capital lens, they are framed as the flexible commodification of self to promote capital production with an end goal measured in purely economic terms. This differs greatly from the original meaning of the term as a tool to disrupt social reproduction and achieve equity.

The work of economist James Heckman (Heckman et al., 2000; Heckman & Katuz, 2012; Heckman & Rubinstein, 2001) is most known for connecting soft skills with labor market "success" and advocating for their use in education as a form of human capital development. In two of their most widely cited studies, Heckman and colleagues (Heckman et al., 2000; Heckman & Rubinstein, 2001) argue the importance of soft skills in determining the outcomes of GED recipients by examining a subsample of 190 White male GED recipients from the 1979–1994 waves of the National Longitudinal Study of Youth (NLSY). Before controlling for certain variables, the data indicate that the subsample of GED recipients have a higher hourly wage ($9.10) than high school dropouts ($8.70) and a lower hourly wage than high school graduates ($10.80).[1] However, after controlling for GED recipients' standardized test scores on the U.S. Armed Forces Qualification Test and the number of years of school they had completed, they found that the hourly wage of GED recipients was actually 9% lower than that of high school dropouts. Heckman and colleagues (2000) conclude that there must be some "unmeasured factor," a "latent dimension of human capital" (p. 1) that caused the difference, which they ultimately identify as "non-cognitive skills."

Heckman et al. (2000) based their conclusion that noncognitive skills (or soft skills) are the reason that GED recipients made less than high school dropouts on a set of "behavior and personality problems" (p. 2) that Heckman et al. determine GED recipients in their sample to exhibit. Specifically, they claim "GED's are 'wiseguys,' who lack the abilities to think ahead, to persist in tasks, or to adapt to their environments" (Heckman & Rubinstein, 2001, p. 146). This claim is based on Heckman and colleagues aligning the family background, employment experience, and self-reported "illegal and delinquent behavior" sections of the NLSY survey with notions of behavior and personality deficits. They conclude that because the GED recipients in their sample reported criminal behavior at higher rates, more often came from "mixed" family backgrounds (i.e., single-parent households), and had less stable employment experiences, they lacked self-discipline and persistence.

Based on their findings, Heckman and Rubinstein (2001) provide recommendations concerning soft skills and educational reforms, such as evaluating educational systems for their "effects on producing the non-cognitive traits that are also valued in the market" (p. 148). Specifically, the economists promote the "effectiveness of Catholic schools" at "producing more motivated and self-disciplined students" and denounce the "decline in discipline in inner-city public schools [as] a major source of their failure" (2001, p. 148). They also recommend that "social policy should be more active in attempting to alter [noncognitive traits], especially for children from disadvantaged environments who receive poor discipline and encouragement at home" (p. 149).

Heckman and Rubinstein's (2001) widely cited recommendations that align with a *human* capital approach strongly contradict the previously discussed *cultural* capital literature, which advocates an asset-oriented understanding of learners' cultural wealth (Gonzáles et al., 2005; Ladson-Billings, 1995; Paris & Alim, 2014; Yosso, 2005). Instead, these arguments adhere to the aforementioned cultural deficit model by locating "failure" within marginalized individuals and/or their communities and overlooking root causes of oppression. Heckman and Rubinstein blame GED recipients' lack of "success in life" on perceived character inadequacies and families' deficits and support their arguments by referring to personal cultural beliefs (i.e., the effectiveness of Catholic schools) and stereotypes (i.e., inner-city schoolchildren need more discipline).

Standardizing and Assessing Soft Skills

Since Heckman and colleagues' (2000) widely cited GED study, the use of "noncognitive" intelligence measures and/or personality assessments within econometrics has become increasingly common (Almund et al., 2011; Deming, 2017; Duckworth et al., 2007; Heckman & Kautz, 2012). Econometric analyses that use such assessments generally conceptualize "personality traits" as "predictors and causes of academic and economic success, health, and criminal activity" (Almund et al., 2011, p. 3) by attempting to tie such assessments and/or trait taxonomies to economic productivity (Almund et al., 2011; Duckworth et. al, 2007; Heckman & Kautz, 2012). Yet economists have struggled to understand the self-reported nature of most psychology-developed personality assessments and have pushed for more standardized assessments that can be used as educational metrics to determine student performance (Deming, 2017; Heckman, & Kautz, 2011). This has led to a significant growth in efforts to develop standardized definitions, taxonomies, and assessments for soft skills. For example, the Ecological Approaches to Social Emotional Learning (EASEL) Laboratory in Harvard's School of Education recently began a project titled "The Taxonomy Project: Non-Cognitive Skills for Learning and Life" that aims to "generate a coherent taxonomy of non-cognitive skills" to better define, measure, and compare these skills for educational policymakers, researchers, and funders (Jones, n.d., "What Is the Taxonomy Project?"). Likewise, the U.S. National Research Council (2011) has also been developing assessments of "21st-century skills," which aim to define and test problem-solving, critical thinking, communication, flexibility, self-management, and independent learning.

Critiques of Human Capital Framings of Soft Skills

It is important to question the value and the validity of standardized definitions and measurements of soft skills. Do such taxonomies truly reflect how such skills are understood and used both in and out of the workplace? And do they incorporate all the potential uses, outcomes, and purposes for such skills and competencies? A limited, but growing, body of scholarship has begun critiquing soft skills discourses by locating them within a particular understanding of the self and society (Asher Golden, 2015; Choo, 2017; Gershon, 2011; Urciuoli, 2008; Walkerdine, 2005). These critiques emphasize how dominant conceptualizations of the self within the idea of soft skills lack ethical consideration, limit educational possibilities, and overly prioritize workplace competencies (Choo, 2017). Likewise, the neoliberal framing of soft skills causes people to begin to see themselves as small corporations and see their relationships with other people as either market alliances or competition with other selves as corporations. Furthermore, this framing conceptualizes a school as the location of the market exchange of time/money for skills and credentials for the self-corporation that must constantly seek productivity. These "selves as corporations" then embody a collection of skills and traits that are reflexively monitored, developed, and customized to meet market needs (Gershon, 2011). Thus, a person's sense of self is increasingly based on their work and on their ability to be consumers of what they sell (Walkerdine, 2005).

Critiques of soft skills discourses bring up important questions concerning what constitutes "right," "good" behavior; who decides this behavior; and how society determines and manages such behavior. According to the dominant soft skill conceptualization, "good" behavior is something that results in economic prosperity. However, it is important to examine the underlying logic of these universalized recommendations as well as alternative understandings of these conceptualizations. Nursing, like teaching, is a particularly useful occupation to examine these questions because nursing is an occupation where soft skills are most essential to the job. This is not only because of the interpersonal tasks required in nursing but also because of the high stakes involved in the profession. Therefore, a deeper understanding of how such a profession describes soft skills adds a tremendous amount to our understanding of how such skills are actually understood and enacted in day-to-day life. In fact, the former and future nurses who participated in this study describe soft skills much differently from most economists using a human capital lens. Participants brought up ideas related to caring, love, compassion, and empathy, which are not viewed through human capital ideology as having "market value." These findings question the adequacy and rationale for the dominant soft skill narratives and taxonomies based on research examining the market return of soft skills.

Research Methodology

The findings presented in this chapter draw on qualitative interview data with nursing educators and nursing students regarding the skills, competencies, and abilities they believed people most needed in their profession with special attention to their conceptualization and usage of communication, teamwork, problem-solving, and self-directed learning skills. Data were collected in 2017 at a highly competitive school of nursing in a large U.S. city. We randomly recruited thirty-six participants from a Bachelor of Science in Nursing program, including two administrators, nine instructors, and 25 students (see Table 8.1). All administrator and instructor participants were also former nurses. The majority of participants self-identified as female (94%) and White (64%). These demographics are consistent with the gender demographics of Registered Nurses (RNs) nationally, which are 91% women, and relatively consistent with the racial and ethnic demographics of RNs nationally, which are 75% White (Minority Nurse, 2015). The implications of these demographics are discussed further in the discussion section.

Table 8.1. Participant Self-Identified Demographic Characteristics

	Total	Average Age	Total Female	Total Male	Total Asian or Asian American	Total Hispanic or Latino/a	Total Black or African American	Total White or Caucasian
Nursing Educators	11	57	11	0	1	1	1	8
Nursing Students	25	28	23	2	2	5	3	15
Total Participants	**36**	**36**	**34**	**2**	**3**	**6**	**4**	**23**

Administrators and instructors participated in individual semistructured interviews while students participated in a three- to five-person focus group interview. Interviews and focus groups lasted approximately 45 to 60 minutes and focused on why participants entered the nursing field; the skills, competencies, knowledge, and abilities they think nurses need; and how they think those skills, competencies, knowledge, and abilities are best taught. Participants were asked to write down single words or short phrases that came to mind immediately when they thought about the skills and competencies essential for students to acquire before they graduate from their nursing program. After finishing writing, participants were asked to elaborate on what they considered to be the most important competency on that list. Then participants were asked a series of questions pertaining specifically to communication, problem-solving, teamwork, and self-directed learning. These questions were designed to capture how participants defined and taught, or were being taught, these skills.

All interviews were transcribed and entered into NVivo qualitative data analysis software, whereupon members of the research team segmented the raw data into more manageable units based on participants' background and associated research questions. The author of this article along with another member of the research team then thematically analyzed the data to better understand the skills participants believed nurses most need (Saldaña, 2012). Several cycles of coding took place that involved numerous analytic memos to document emerging themes. Analysts were also in constant conversation with one another concerning the emerging themes as well as any instances of discrepant evidence or negative cases in order to ensure reliability. Limitations of the study include the generally small, self-selected sample and the lack of multiple interviews.

Findings

In their discussion of the skills, competencies, knowledge, and abilities nurses need, nursing educators and students highlighted and described understandings of soft skills that do not fit the dominant conceptualizations. A significant portion of their discussions included humanizing notions of soft skills that related more toward love and compassion than productivity and profit. In particular, participants discussed the importance of the following characteristics rarely (if ever) brought up in the discussions on soft skills: empathy, love, open-mindedness, caring, mindfulness, respect, honesty, humility, trustworthiness, culturally responsiveness, and advocacy. The following section provides key examples of how these humanizing ideas were discussed and analyze their significance.

Empathy, Compassion, and Love

Notions of empathy, compassion, and love were some of the most commonly discussed themes in response to questions concerning the skills, competencies, knowledge, and abilities nurses need. Nursing educators and students consistently highlighted how valuable caring about patients is. For example, Cassidy[2] stated that the first thing that came to her mind when thinking about the skills nurses need was "caring" because "If you don't care for people, then why are you in the profession to begin with?" Likewise, Rachel claimed that "compassion" was "the fundamental quality" of nursing, and Jasmine contended that compassion was a "given in nursing" because "you work with a lot of people who are vulnerable, they are sick, they depend on you. So you need that compassion to do the work that you should do."

Additionally, Katie, a recent nursing school graduate and practicing nurse stated nurses need to be "able to love [their] patients regardless of where they came from, whether they're like you or not, you agree with how they live or not . . . nursing is really about being there for the patient." She also added that the "skill" of empathy may not be something that someone can necessarily be taught, saying that "it's something you either have or you don't have." This brings up important questions about how an individual's personal values and life experiences influence their career paths and professional lives. For example, Patricia decided to go back to school to become a nurse because she always "had the desire to take care of people," saying that being a nurse is more about "fulfillment" than "to make money" and that she does not want "a job" but "a career" in which she can "feel like [she's] making a difference." Therefore, notions of "success," according to Patricia, had much more to do with personal gratification than economic gains.

Advocacy and Ethics

To participants, a significant part of "making a difference" involved performing the role of patient advocate. Joyce Mori, an assistant professor of nursing, explained that nurses do not just receive orders, but rather, they are responsible for "reviewing the treatment plan to make sure that it's best for the patient" because "we are advocating for the patient." Professor Mori considered this to be a "societal responsibility" of nurses that required strong ethics. Important aspects of those ethics that emerged in the data were the ideas of "respect" and "trust." For example, another nursing professor told us that "respectfulness, trustworthiness . . . and dignity" were some of the most important "skills" a nurse needs, while nursing students Alejandra and Jasmine discussed the importance of developing trust with patients. Many participants also discussed the importance of honesty. Nursing professor Melissa Thompson even stated that "if you're not honest in your communication and you're just being politically correct about it, you're not helping the situation." Part of being an advocate also involved being honest and speaking up about difficult matters, such as mistakes. For example, Hailey said that "sometimes you're going to make a mistake or you're going to see somebody else make a mistake . . . and a mistake could cost a life so you need to be able to feel comfortable to speak up." Thus, even though ideas concerning advocacy, social responsibility, and ethics are lacking in popular discussions about soft skills, they seemed to be key to our participants.

The "Whole" Patient

Another dominant theme that emerged when discussing the skills, competencies, knowledge, and abilities nurses need was the idea of looking at the "whole patient." Associate professor Debra Romano (age 63; White) discussed the importance of nurses "looking at the whole patient" in terms of understanding all the patients' medications, conditions, and medical history to not overlook anything. Nursing student Alejandra added to this idea by saying that nurses have to "think of the patient as a person and look at them holistically." She stated that nurses are not only taking care of a patient's body, but they also "have to take care of their spirituality, emotion, and everything else." This idea was echoed by many other participants who claimed that nurses are not just there to "take care of the disease but the person" and that nurses are "not just treating the physical parts but also the psychological."

According to nursing professor Dolores Lipman, part of her approach to achieving a holistic understanding of patient needs involved the idea of mindfulness. She stated that when she is with a patient, she wants them to know that "when I'm with you, I'm with you. I'm not thinking about what I'm going to cook for dinner tonight or what's going on emotionally for me, but I'm in that present time." Other participants also discussed the importance of general "awareness" with respect to power dynamics between nurses and patients, patients and their family members, and nurses and other medical professionals. Again, this idea of being present and mindful is rarely, if ever, brought up in common conversations concerning soft skills. Likewise, it is highly unlikely that these sorts of ideas could be standardized and measured in the ways that many soft skills proponents suggest.

Communication Is More Than Words

In discussing communication skills within nursing, participants brought up many aspects of communication that are not always discussed within the general literature on communication as a soft skill. To participants, strong communication skills involved much more than words. Participants discussed ideas concerning nonverbal communication, such as the importance of touch and general rapport. Professor Clair Norman, who has been a nurse educator for 26 years, stated:

> You've got to be communicating with the patient in the way you work, the way you walk, your presence where you are. I mean, you can be communicating, caring, I'm watching you, I'm not going to let anything bad happen to you, I'm giving you your space. Whatever you're trying to communicate just

> by where you are with respect to the patient's' bedside. So it's an intangible level of communication as well as verbal or touch. Touching is very important in nursing. You can convey sympathy or caring or any number of emotions just by how you touch a patient.

The idea of communicating through one's presence was echoed by other participants. Nursing student Kristin explained that communicating can be "verbal, facial expressions, or touch," and Professor Gutierrez pointed out that a patient "feels your energy" as soon as the nurse walks into the room. Likewise, Professor Romano defined a good communicator as "one who connects through eye contact, hears what a person says, asks what they need to ask, and gathers all of the information." Listening was also brought up as a key component to "good" communication skills in nursing. Another nursing student stated that during her clinicals, she has noticed that "you have to listen to see what's coming next . . . and learn to listen to everything that's in your surroundings." These understandings of the embodied nature of communication are also not typically brought up in the literature on soft skills, nor are they "skills" that could be easily assessed through the means in which many soft skills proponents propose.

Finally, another key idea that came up in discussing communication skills within nursing was being able to communicate with varied interlocutors and audiences. This included being able to translate medical jargon into layperson's terms, deliver delicate news to patients and their families, and accurately convey information to other medical professionals. Additionally, this idea also involved a strong level of cultural competency. For example, nursing student Anna brought up the importance of communicating with "different types of people," while Professor Lipman discussed the need to be able to communicate with patients "of all cultures and educational levels."

Discussion

These findings suggest that soft skills are unfixed and culturally variable depending on individual and group values, priorities, goals, and life experiences. The nursing educators and students who participated in this study reported caring, compassion, and mindfulness as some of the most important skills, competencies, knowledge, and abilities for nurses to possess. These findings provide an understanding of the forms of cultural capital (Bourdieu & Passeron, 1977) valued within the nursing profession, as well as an understanding of why these forms are valued. Participants stated that these were the most important skills for nurses to have to provide the best possible care to patients as well as to fulfill a personal desire to help others. These findings contradict the more commonly promoted human capital understandings of soft skills and problematize designs to standardize and measure soft skills.

The voices and perspectives presented in this analysis are predominantly women involved in a "caring profession" (e.g., nursing, teaching, childcare work, social work). Within feminist literature, particularly literature on women in caring professions, the topic of care and caring is a prominent theme (Abel, Nelson, & Nelson, 1990); Meyer, 2002, Thomas; 1993). While a detailed discussion of this literature, as well as its history, debates, and nuances, is beyond the scope of this chapter, it is significant to point the absence of the perspectives of women in caring professions within soft skills discourses. While this absence is not surprising given the general marginalization of women and the low societal value placed on the caring professions (Babic & Gault, 2016; Bunting, 2016), the lack of inclusion of these perspectives within soft skill discussions provides an overlooked form of community knowledge and cultural capital. This significant omission brings up important questions regarding if (and how) the soft skills considered important by women in caring professions are being valued.

In examining economists Heckman and Rubinstein's (2001) assertion that educational systems should be evaluated based on their "effects on producing the non-cognitive traits that are also valued in the market" (p. 148), one can discern that the noncognitive traits espoused by the participants in this study would not be included because ideas such as compassion, love, and caring are not considered "valuable" within a free-market rationale. Likewise, Heckman and Rubinstein also recommend that "social policy should be more active in attempting to alter [noncognitive traits], especially for children from disadvantaged environments who receive poor discipline and encouragement at home" (2001, p. 149). But their determination of whose soft skills need to be altered is a largely gendered, raced, and classed judgment that favors privileged White, male, middle-class norms with which the authors seem to personally agree without consideration of the types of soft skills espoused by the nursing educators and students presented in this study.

According to educational researcher Tara Yosso (2005), cultural capital "refers to an accumulation of specific forms of knowledge, skills, and abilities that are valued by privileged groups in society" (p. 76). In many ways, the current conceptualization of "soft skills" promotes a universalized standard of cultural capital that is considered *good* and *right* by a particular privileged outlook. While there is no one "right" personality trait or interpersonal disposition, the "right" way that is currently being advocated is based on a very particular moral code—that of human capital. Furthermore, the imposition of that particular moral code on nurses, "children from disadvantaged environments" (Heckman & Rubinstein, 2001, p. 149), or anyone else constitutes a form of symbolic violence in which dominant groups attempt to ingrain their cultural values on the dominated, thereby contributing to the continuation of social reproduction (Bourdieu & Passeron, 1977).

According to Bourdieu and Passeron (1977), the educational system is a very important agent when it comes to legitimizing dominant power structures and exercising symbolic violence. Part of Zwerling's (1976) original argument concerning soft skills pertained to the related notion of educating low-income students about the dominant power structures as an attempt to increase critical awareness and combat mechanisms of social reproduction. Yet current soft skill discourses do not attempt to teach *about* dominant power structures; rather, they attempt to teach *to* those structures by presenting soft skills as acceptable, normal, neutral behavior. The normalization of this process is further strengthened by the ongoing attempt to standardize and measure soft skills and use them as predictors for future life outcomes. Such research should give pause to educators and educational policy makers interested in cultural plurality and educational equity.

Conclusion

The increased attention on soft skills education comes from a human capital logic that emphasizes economic profit and productivity within global capitalism. The goals of this outlook are to create flexible workers with transferable skills to meet market demands. However, it is important for educators (of PK–12 students, teachers and nurses in training, etc.) to ask if this is truly what human beings and their societies need. Personal attributes, personality traits, and interpersonal dispositions should not be standardized and assessed. No one has the right to standardize such personal aspects, nor does anyone have the right to include them as part of an assessed curriculum. Such standardizations and assessments commodify humanity by trying to coopt deeply innate and intimate human emotions and ways of being for profit. For the nursing educators and students who participated in this study, soft skills did not equate to economic gains. Rather, they indicted the deeply human relationships nurses have with patients. For the former and future nurses who participated in this study, soft skills meant the ability to show compassion, connect with patients, convey care and love through nonverbal communication, and be mindful and patient. Such nondominant forms of cultural capital must be recognized and embraced as valid and valuable forms of soft skills. Acknowledgment of these forms draws attention to the inadequacy of dominant soft skill narratives and taxonomies that focus entirely on the market return of soft skills. It is important to recognize the plurality of soft skills conceptualizations and reject uniform notions to maintain and explore multiple worldviews and ways of being.

Notes

1. In 1993 U.S. dollars.
2. All people and place names have been changed to protect confidentiality.

References

Abel, E. K., Nelson, M. K., & Nelson, M. K. (Eds.). (1990). *Circles of care: Work and identity in women's lives*. SUNY Press.

Almund, M., Duckworth, A. L., Heckman, J., & Kautz, T. (2011). Personality psychology and economics. In E. Hanushek & F. Welch (Eds.). *Handbook of the economics of education* (Vol. 4, pp. 1–181). Elsevier.

Anyon, J. (1997). *Ghetto schooling: A political economy of urban educational reform*. Teachers College Press.

Apple, M. W. (1982). *Education and power*. Routledge & Kegan Paul.

Asher Golden, N. (2015). "There's still that window that's open": The problem with "grit." *Urban Education, 52*(3), 343–369.

Babic, M., & Gault, B. (2016). *The economy undervalues "women's work," and that needs to change*. PBS.org. https://www.pbs.org/newshour/economy/column-economy-undervalues-womens-work-needs-change

Bartlett, L. (2007). Bilingual literacies, social identification, and educational trajectories. *Linguistics and Education: An International Research Journal, 18*(3–4), 215–231.

Becker, G. S. (1983). *Human capital: A theoretical and empirical analysis, with special reference to education* (2nd ed.). University of Chicago Press.

Bourdieu, P. (1986) The forms of capital. In J. Richardson (Ed.), *Handbook of theory and research for the sociology of education* (pp. 241–258). Greenwood.

Bourdieu, P., & Passeron, J. C. (1977). *Reproduction in education, society and culture*. Sage Publications.

Bowles, S., & Gintis, H. (1976). *Schooling in capitalist America: Educational reform and the contradictions of economic life*. Basic Books.

Bunting, M. (2016). Who cares: The emotional labour of an undervalued, underpaid workforce. *The Guardian*. https://www.theguardian.com/society/2016/mar/15/care-workers-undervalued-underpaid-radio-3

Buras, K. (2011). Race, charter schools, and conscious capitalism: On the spatial politics of whiteness as property (and the unconscionable assault on Black New Orleans). *Harvard Educational Review, 81*(2), 296–331.

Choo, S. (2018). Approaching twenty-first century education from a cosmopolitan perspective, *Journal of Curriculum Studies, 50*(2), 162–181.

Conchas, G. Q. (2006). *The color of school success: Race and high-achieving urban youth*. Teachers College Press.

Delgado Gaitán, C. (2001). *The power of community: Mobilizing for family and schooling*. Rowan & Littlefield.

Deming, D. J. (2017.) The growing importance of social skills in the labor market. *The Quarterly Journal of Economics, 132*(4), 1593–1640.

Duckworth, A. L., Peterson, C., Matthews, M. D., & Kelly, D. R. (2007). Grit: Perseverance and passion for long-term goals. *Journal of Personality and Social Psychology, 92*(6), 1087–1101.

Gallavan, M., Truex, D., & Kvasny, L. (2004). Changing patterns in IT skill sets 1988–2003: a content analysis of classified advertisements. *The Database for Advances Systems, 35*(1), 64–87

Gay, G. (2000). *Culturally responsive teaching: Theory, research, and practice*. Teachers College Press.

Gershon, I. (2011). "Neoliberal agency." *Current Anthropology, 52*(4), 537–555.

Giroux, H. A. (1981). *Ideology, culture & the process of schooling*. Temple University Press and Farmer Press.

Gonzáles, N., Moll, L., & Amanti, C. (2005). *Funds of knowledge: Theorizing practices in households, communities, and classrooms*. Erlbaum.

Heckman, J. J., Hsee, J. H., & Rubinstein, Y. (2000). *The GED is a "mixed signal": The effect of cognitive and non-cognitive skills on human capital and labor market outcomes* (Working paper). University of Chicago.

Heckman, J. J., & Kautz, T. (2012). Hard evidence on soft skills. *Labour Economics, 19*(4), 451–464.

Heckman, J. J., & Rubinstein, Y. (2001). The importance of noncognitive skills: Lessons from the GED testing program. *The American Economic Review, 91*(2), 145–149.

Hora, M. T., Benbow, R. J., & Oleson, A. K. (2016). *Beyond the skills gap: Preparing college students for life and work*. Harvard Education Press.

Jones, S. M. (n.d.). *The taxonomy project.* https://easel.gse.harvard.edu/files/gse-easel-lab/files/taxonomy_handout_0.pdf

Ladson-Billings, G. (1995). Toward a theory of culturally relevant pedagogy. *American Educational Research Journal, 32*(3), 465–491.

Meyer, M. H. (Ed.). (2002). *Care work: Gender, labor, and the welfare state.* Routledge.

Minority Nurse. (2015). *Nursing statistics.* Springer Publishing. https://minoritynurse.com/nursing-statistics/

Moeller, K. (2018). *The gender effect: Capitalism, feminism, and the corporate politics of development.* University of California Press.

National Research Council. (2011). *Assessing 21st century skills: Summary of a workshop.* National Academies Press.

Paris, D. & Alim, H.S. (2014). What are you seeking to sustain through culturally sustaining pedagogy? A loving critique forward. *Harvard Educational Review, 84*(1), 85–100.

Saldaña, J. (2012). *The coding manual for qualitative researchers.* Thousand Oaks, CA: Sage.

Schultz, T. (1961). Investment in human capital. *The American Economic Review, 51*(1), 1–17.

Spring, J. H. (2015). *Economization of education: Human capital, global corporations, skills-based schooling.* Routledge.

Steele, C. M. (1997). A threat in the air: How stereotypes shape intellectual identity and performance. *American Psychologist, 52*(6), 613–629.

Thomas, C. (1993). De-constructing concepts of care. *Sociology, 27*(4), 649–669.

Urciuoli, B. (2008). Skills and selves in the new workplace. *American Ethnologist, 35*(2), 211–228.

Valenzuela, A. (1999). *Subtractive schooling: US–Mexican youth and the politics of caring.* State University of New York Press.

Walkerdine, V. (2005, Spring). Freedom, psychology, and the neoliberal worker. *Soundings: A Journal of Politics and Culture, 29*, 47–61.

Yosso, T. J. (2005). Whose culture has capital? A critical race theory discussion of community cultural wealth. *Race Ethnicity and Education, 8*(1), 69–91.

Zwerling, L. S. (1976). *Second best: The crisis of the community college.* McGraw-Hill.

EDITOR AND CONTRIBUTOR BIOGRAPHIES

Editors

T. JAMESON BREWER, PHD, is an assistant professor of social foundations of education at the University of North Georgia. His teaching experience spans from the middle school, high school, undergraduate, master's, and doctoral levels. Broadly conceptualized, his research focuses on the impact of privatization and marketization of public education by way of school vouchers, charter schools, alternative teacher certification, and homeschooling. His most recent books are *Philanthropy, Strategy, and Collective Resistance: A Primer for Educators* (Myers Education Press, 2019), *Learning to Teach in an Era of Privatization: Global Trends in Teacher Preparation* (Teachers College Press, 2019), and *Teach For All Counter-Narratives: International Perspectives on a Global Reform Movement* (Peter Lang, 2020). Follow him on Twitter: @tjamesonbrewer.

W. GREGORY HARMAN, EDD, MEA, is an associate professor of teacher education at Lewis-Clark State College. He was formerly at Dominican University, Chicago. He teaches educational psychology, educational philosophy, and social studies methods and mentors teacher candidates in student teaching. He began in education as a social studies teacher, teaching middle and high school students for over a decade in the Twin Cities metro. He has edited for *SOJO*, reviewed for *Education Policy Analysis Archives*, and has published in both as well as in *Educational Theory, Teaching with Primary Sources: Research & Practice, Critical Questions in Education*, and *Teaching & Learning*.

Contributors

ASHLEE B. ANDERSON, PHD, holds a doctorate in education with a primary specialization in cultural studies in education and a secondary specialization in education leadership and policy studies from the University of Tennessee, Knoxville. She is currently a clinical associate professor within the Department of Theory and Practice in Teacher Education, also at the University of Tennessee. Her primary research interests are foundations of education/sociology of education, teacher education/teacher development, qualitative research methodologies, education policy and reform, international education, equity and social justice, and cultural studies in education.

ANDREA ARCE-TRIGATTI, PHD, is an interdisciplinary educational researcher and evaluator interested in diversity, equity, cultural studies, and social justice issues in engineering education, pedagogy, and educational policy. She is a founding member of the award-winning Renaissance Foundry Research Group, developing and investigating the pedagogical techniques utilized to enhance critical and creative thinking at interdisciplinary interfaces. Working with underrepresented, rural, and first-generation student populations, she is also involved with several research to practice projects centering on student representation, community outreach, student success, and resilience, as well as pedagogical practices for holistic learning.

SCOTT T. GRUBBS is an instructor in the Division of Education at Thomas University. During his three decades in education, he has been a high school French teacher, high school department head, and university faculty. Additionally, he has served as council for the accreditation of educator preparation coordinator, accreditation review chair, co-chair of the Evaluation Review Panel for the Georgia Professional Standards Commission, and an accreditation consultant. His primary research interests are educational politics, educational policy, rural education, program evaluation, and accreditation.

MICHELLE STRATER GUNDERSON is a 34-year teaching veteran who currently teaches first grade in the Chicago Public Schools. As a union leader, she serves as a vice president of the Illinois Federation of Teachers and as a trustee for the Chicago Teachers Union and is the former co-chair of CORE (Caucus of Rank and File Educators).

MATTHEW J. HAYDEN, PHD, is an associate professor of education and the director of SOE International Programs at Drake University. He teaches undergraduate and graduate courses in educational foundations, educational psychology, ethics, honors, and a doctoral seminar about the philosophy and theories of education. His research is framed by ethics and moral philosophy, psychology, and sociology applied to education and schooling. He earned his PhD from Teachers College, Columbia University, and received the 2012 Kuhmerker Dissertation Award from the Association for Moral Education. His recent publications include "Disemboweling Education: Killing Living Labor With Technocratic Commodification" (2018), *The SoJo Journal: Educational Foundations and Social Justice Education, 5*(1).

DENISHA JONES, PHD, is the director of the Art of Teaching Program at Sarah Lawrence College. She received a bachelor's degree in early childhood education from the University of the District of Columbia in 2003. Denisha worked as a kindergarten teacher and a preschool director before spending the past 17 years as a teacher educator. She earned her PhD in curriculum and instruction from Indiana University in 2013. In 2018, she earned her Juris Doctor from the David A. Clarke School of Law at the University of the District of Columbia.

MICHAEL SCHAD, PHD, is an instructional designer and researcher at Virginia Commonwealth University. He is a former middle school English teacher and his research focuses on science, technology, engineering, math, and the integration of the maker movement in educational institutions.

BAILEY B. SMOLAREK, PHD, is an associate researcher with the Wisconsin Center for Education Research at the University of Wisconsin–Madison. Bailey holds a PhD in curriculum and instruction and specializes in language and education, education policy studies, and qualitative research. Drawing on critical social theories, Bailey's scholarship revolves around issues of educational equity from both systemic and localized understandings. Informed by her prior roles as a Spanish and English as a Second Language teacher, Bailey is dedicated to research that cultivates socially just educational spaces for multilingual and multicultural learners. Her current work consists community-based participatory action research projects with college students from minoritized backgrounds.

KURT STEMHAGEN, PHD, is a professor of education at Virginia Commonwealth University. He is a former middle school mathematics teacher, and his primary areas of scholarship are democratic theory, mathematics education, and teacher empowerment.

INDEX

accountability, xi, xiii, xv, xvi, 1, 4, 6, 8, 16, 17, 18, 34, 42–43, 48, 59, 66, 70, 79, 81, 85, 87, 89–90, 94, 97–99, 127

A Nation at Risk, 4, 10, 63, 64

Baldwin, James, 74–75, 77

business model, xii–xiii, xv, 1, 3, 4, 8, 127, 129

businessification, xii

charter school, 125–126, 128, 130–134, 137–138

child well being, 46

childhood, xv, 1, 39–51, 54–58

commodification, xvii, 3, 5–8, 14, 16, 27, 34, 40–41, 51, 56, 63, 74, 79, 88–89, 107–108, 120, 122, 126, 139, 146

Commodity, 5, 18, 40, 65–66, 70, 72, 74–75, 80, 88, 90, 107–111, 114–115, 119, 146

COVID-19, xv, 72
- pandemic, xvi, 56

credentialism, 1, 8, 10, 83

cultural capital, 15, 142, 144–145, 146, 148, 157, 158, 159

curriculum, xi, xii, xv, xvi, xvii, 3, 6, 16, 29, 32, 42–43, 48, 55, 69–71, 77, 95, 104, 109, 119–121, 126, 159

Dewey, John, 21, 117–118

discourse, xv, 1, 7, 8, 40, 76, 93, 105, 141–143, 149, 157, 159

education (definitions of), 15, 17, 20–24

essentialism/essentialist (educational essentialism), xv, 7, 8, 14, 15–16, 20

experientialism/experientialist, 14, 19, 21, 42

exploitation, xiv, xvii, 3, 94, 110

GERM (Global Education Reform Movement), 1, 8, 39–42, 48, 49, 51–55, 57

hidden curriculum, xvii, 29

holism/holist, 14, 19, 77, 98, 99, 114, 154, 156, 164

human capital, xv, 2, 142, 145–147, 149, 150, 157, 158

Maker Movement, 1, 107–108, 111–113, 115, 117–118, 120–122

market paradigm, xii, xiv

marketization, 80, 90, 110, 163

merit/meritocracy, 1, 28–29, 49, 64–65, 68–70, 72, 77, 80

neo-essentialism/neo-essentialist, 1, 8, 14, 16, 17–19, 20, 27, 34

neoconservative, 8

neoliberalism, xii, xiii, xvi, xvii, 1, 40, 90, 93, 98
- neoliberal, xii, xiv, xv, xvi, 8, 39, 49, 52, 56–57, 71, 87–90, 93–94, 98–99, 101–102, 104, 108, 119, 149

new managerialism, 8, 88, 89–91, 101

paradigm, xi, xiii, xiv, xv, 1, 3, 4, 6, 7, 8, 71, 76, 88, 92, 93, 105, 110, 111
pedagogy, xiii, 39, 41, 54–58, 89, 102, 104, 164
perennialist/perennialism, 14, 15
personhood, xiii–xiv
play, 34, 39–42, 46–48, 50–52, 54–58, 88, 109
    true play, 41–42, 50–52, 54, 57–58
policy, xii, xvi, 3, 6–7, 19, 27, 34, 43, 45, 63–69, 72–73, 75, 80, 94–95, 98–100, 121, 147, 149, 158–159, 164

responsibility, xi, xiii, 45, 154

school (definitions of), 15, 17–18, 24–25
skill(s), xiv, 2, 17–18, 20, 32, 34, 41–43, 45, 47, 55, 58, 66, 77, 96, 99, 103, 114–115, 134, 141–160
smartness, 1, 63, 65–72, 74–75, 77, 79–81
status quo, xvi, 24, 26, 27, 29, 30, 33, 70, 74, 78
STEM, 27, 118–119
subject/object difference, subjectification/objectification, xiii, xiv, 2–3, 8, 16, 89, 115, 129, 144

trust, 63, 77–80, 132, 136–137, 154

vocational education, 117–118, 121, 143

White Supremacy, xvi